WORKING WITH PAPER

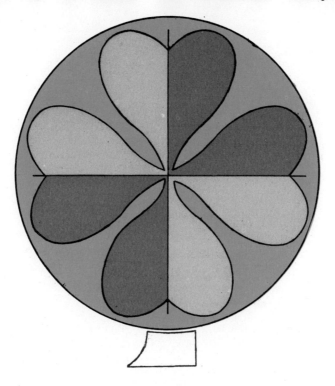

Franklin Watts, Inc
845 Third Avenue
New York, N.Y. 10022

First published October 1969
First English edition 1970
First American publication 1971 by Franklin Watts, Inc.

© 1969 Santillana, S.A. de Ediciones
English translation © 1970, Macdonald & Co. (Publishers) Ltd.

Library of Congress Catalog Card Number: 73-158978

Printed in Spain

Novograph, S. L. Ctra. de Irún, Km. 12,450. Madrid-20.

D.L.M. 14.001/ 71

SBN 531 02003-7

Working with paper

The projects in this book are divided into five grades, from very simple to advanced. The colour key below shows the grades and corresponding symbols, which are repeated at the beginning of each project for easy reference. The very simple projects are designed for younger children but the grades are only intended as a rough guide. Very young children may need some help.

 Very simple

 Easy

 Moderately easy

 More complex

 Advanced

Working with paper is the first volume in the *Colour Crafts* series. It tells you how to make ninety models out of paper. All the projects are illustrated with step-by-step colour pictures and photographs.

The colour-coded square at the beginning of each project tells you how complex each one is, but once you have mastered a few basic techniques of paper handling you should be able to tackle most of the projects in the book. If you get stuck on a model, try another one and go back to the harder one later.

A list of materials is given for each model. It is a good idea to prepare all your materials before you begin. The book covers the use of many types of paper, from magazine cuttings to coloured and silver paper, and you will find the projects even more exciting if you experiment with different kinds of paper. As soon as you have made a few things in the book, you will be able to experiment with other materials too—you can use crayons or paint instead of felt-tip pens, and so on.

Many of the models in this book were made by children. You should try to use the models shown as starting points, and go on to think up your own ideas for different colours, patterns and shapes. Use the index at the back of the book to help you find any particular object you may need.

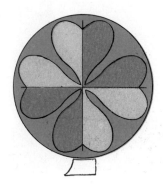

PIN-PRICKING

Get a magazine. Find a picture that you like. Tear out the whole page. You could use scissors to cut the picture. But if you find it hard to use them, try the following:

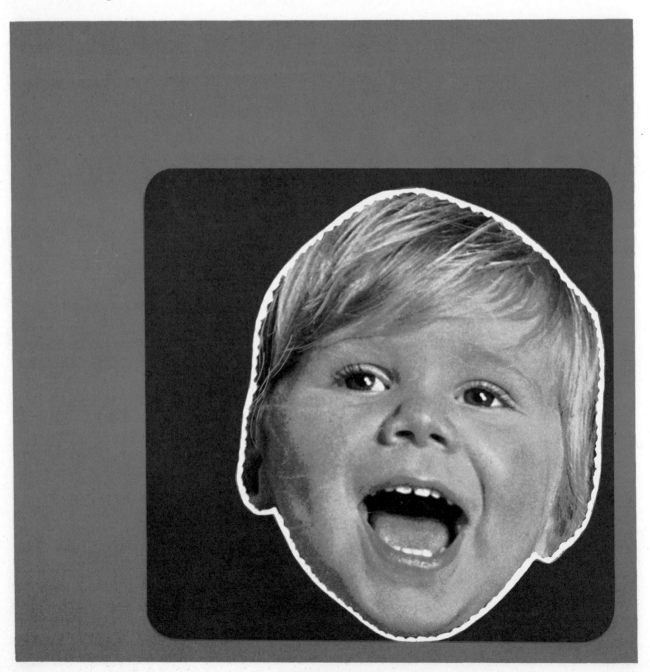

Put the page you have picked on something soft. Prick holes all round the edge of the picture with a pin. Then tear away the rest of the paper bit by bit. Only the picture should be left.

MATERIALS:
- Different coloured cardboard
- Pencil
- Pages from colour magazines

CHRISTMAS CARDS

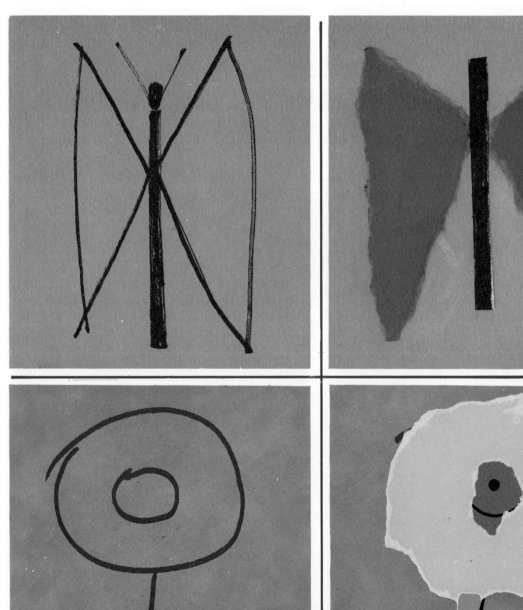

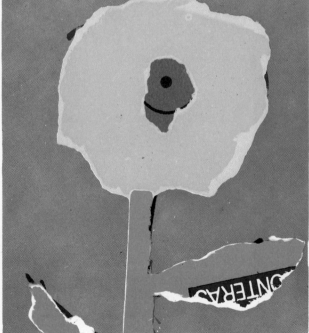

Draw something you like on the pieces of coloured cardboard. On the opposite page is a butterfly and a flower.

Cut pieces from your magazine the same size as your drawings. Now stick them on.

The pictures you see here were made by children of your own age.

They make good Christmas cards.

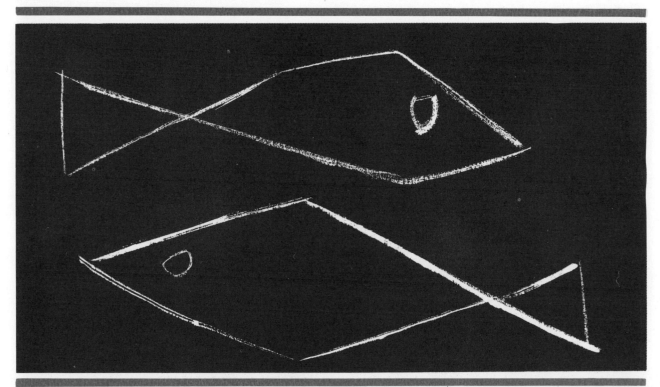

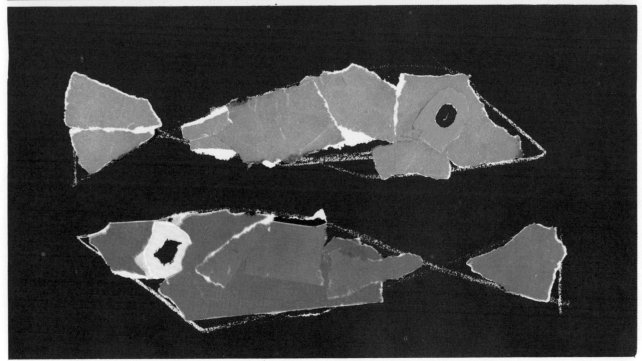

SQUARING PAPER

There are lots of things to make yet. But first you must be able to make a sheet of paper into a square.

This is how to 'square' a long piece of paper.

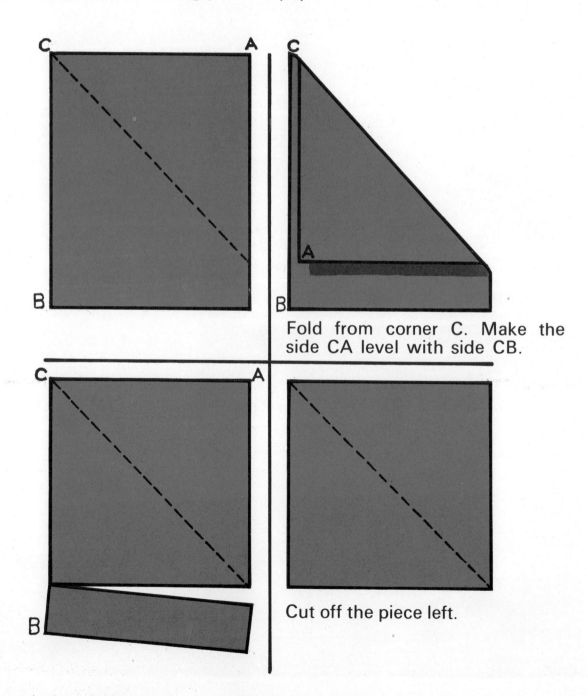

Fold from corner C. Make the side CA level with side CB.

Cut off the piece left.

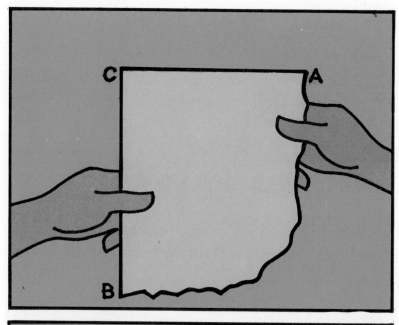

How can you square an odd-shaped piece of paper?

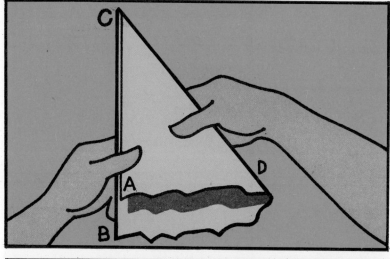

Fold from corner C so that side CA is level with side CB.

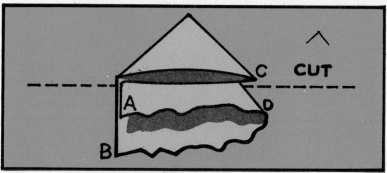

CUT

Fold C over to meet point D.
Cut off what is left.

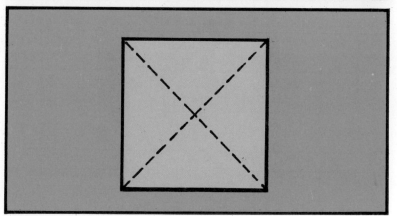

FOLDING PAPER

To make some of the things in this book, you should know how to fold a piece of paper in two ways.

If you are told to fold it this way:

You must:
—Square a sheet of paper
—Fold it from corner to corner
—Fold it again so that point A touches point B.

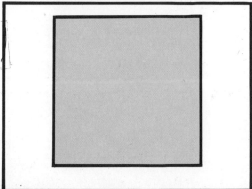

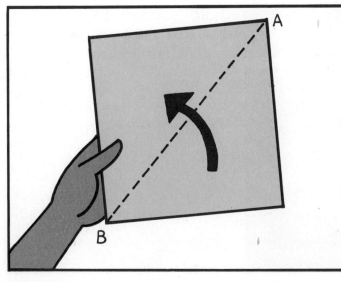

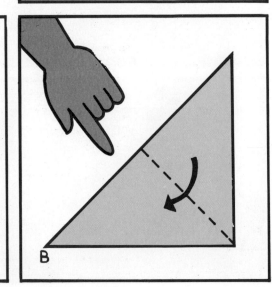

If you are told to fold it this way:

You must:

Square a sheet of paper

Fold it so that A touches B and C touches D

Fold it again so that A touches D.

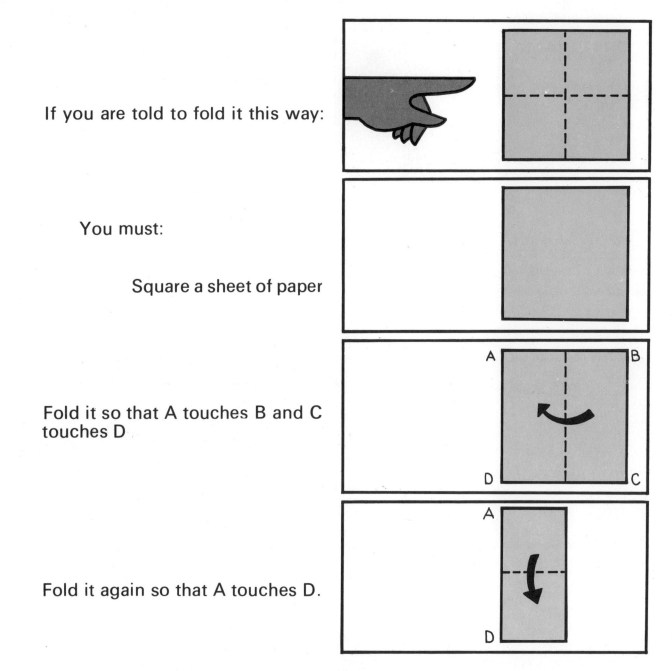

When you can fold and cut, you can make things like birds and boats.

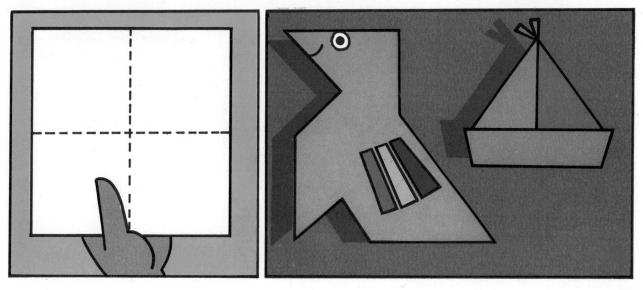

CART

Cut a sheet of paper about 7½in. by 10½in. in half. Take one half and fold it upwards on the dotted lines.

This gives you the base of the cart.

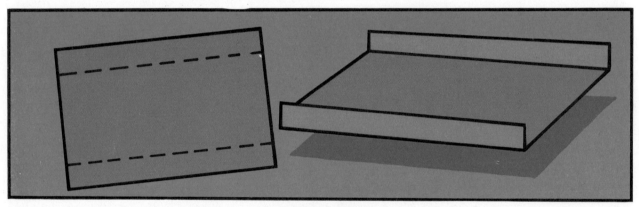

Now take the other half. Bend it as shown.

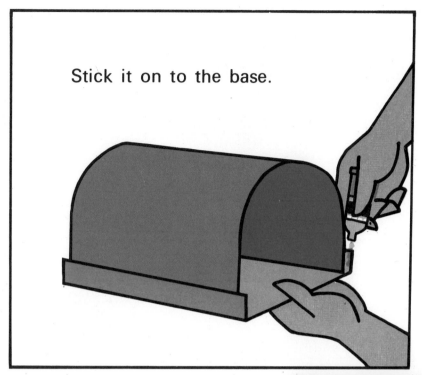

Stick it on to the base.

Put a large coin on a sheet of paper. Draw round it in pencil. Cut out four circles like this blue one to make wheels. Glue them to the cart.

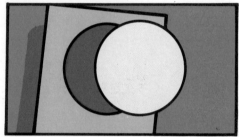

PIN-PRICKING AND TEARING

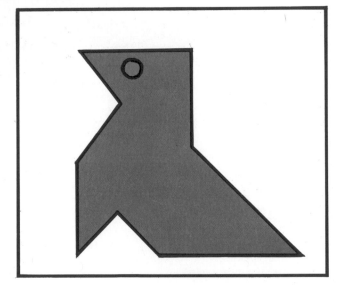

Draw the bird on tracing paper. Put your tracing on a sheet of drawing paper.

Put the sheet of paper on a soft surface. Pin-prick round the bird.

Carefully tear the bird away from the rest of the paper.

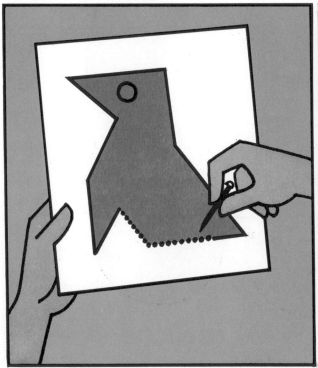

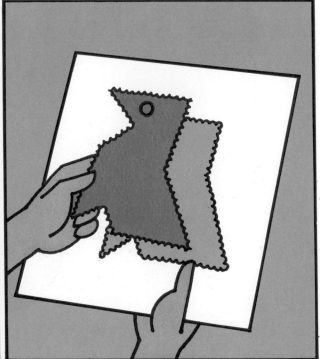

Here are some other shapes.

MATERIALS:

- Paper bag
- Pencil
- Scissors

KING'S MASK

Any paper bag can be turned into a king's mask.

Make a pencil drawing on one side of the bag. You can copy this one.

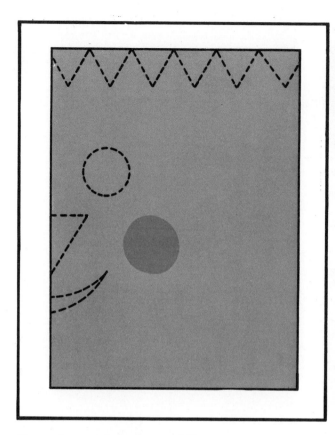

Cut along the dotted lines.

Now you can be a king with the mask you have made.

You can make other masks in the same way.

SNAKES

Cut several long strips about 1in. wide.

Start the snake like this.

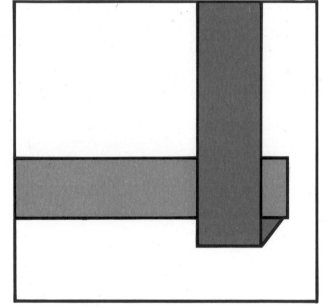

Fold the vertical strip upwards.

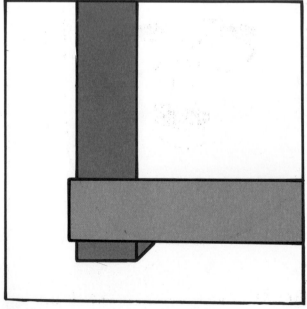

Fold the horizontal strip to the right.

Continue folding the strips one over the other. Glue the ends to stop the snake coming undone.

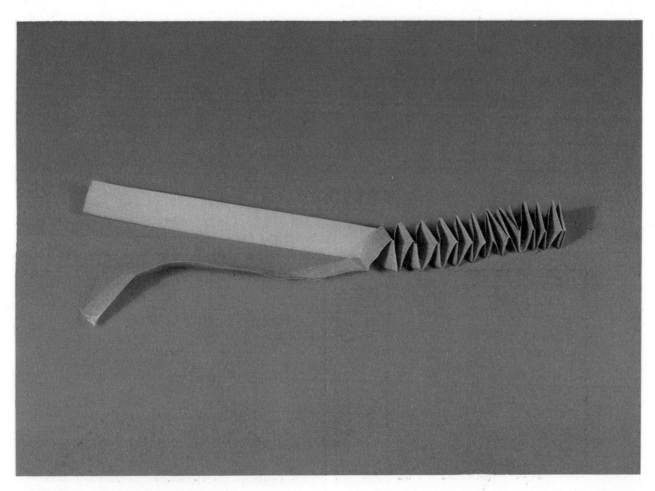

You can make Christmas decorations with these snakes.

You can also make rings. Several rings joined together can be used as a necklace or bracelet.

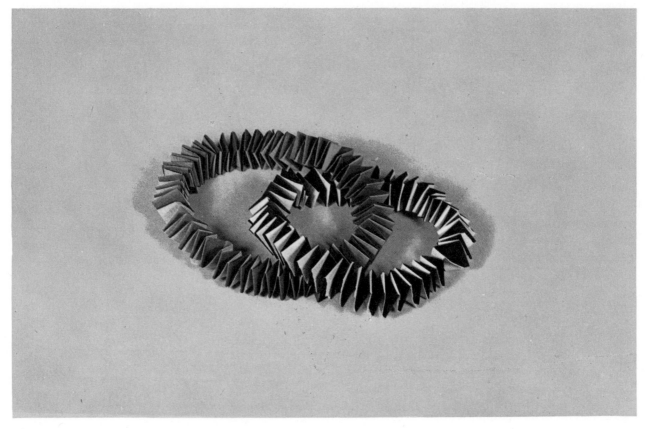

TULIP

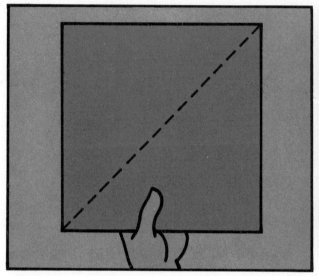

Cut a square out of red paper.
Fold on the dotted line.

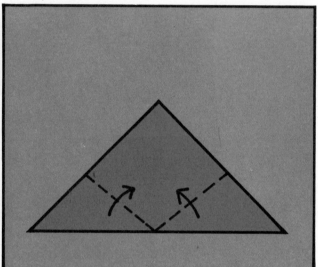

Now fold the corners upwards.

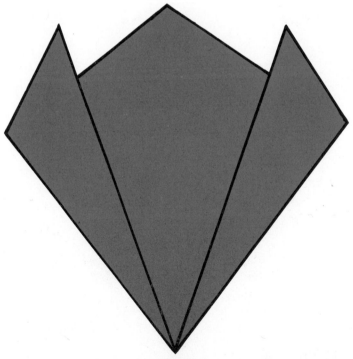

Stick the flower on a large sheet of white paper.

Cut a strip of green paper. Stick it on to
make the stalk. Stick a leaf on each side.

PAPER CHAINS

Cut strips.

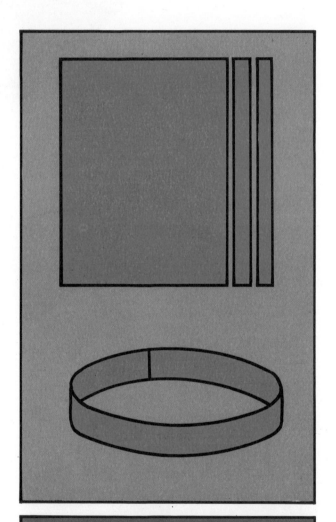

Stick the ends of the first strip together.

Pass the second strip through the ring and stick the ends together.

Do the same with the other strips.

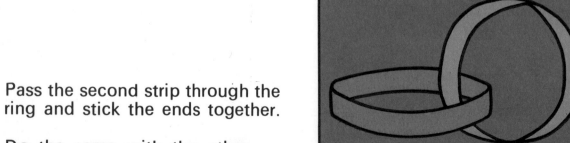

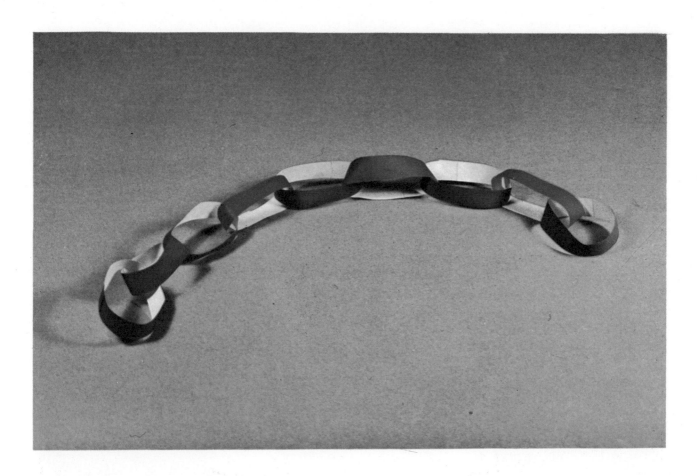

You can make the paper chain with strips of one colour, or you can use different colours. The strips of paper can be cut out of magazines. If you cannot use scissors, tear the paper into strips.

MORE PIN-PRICKING

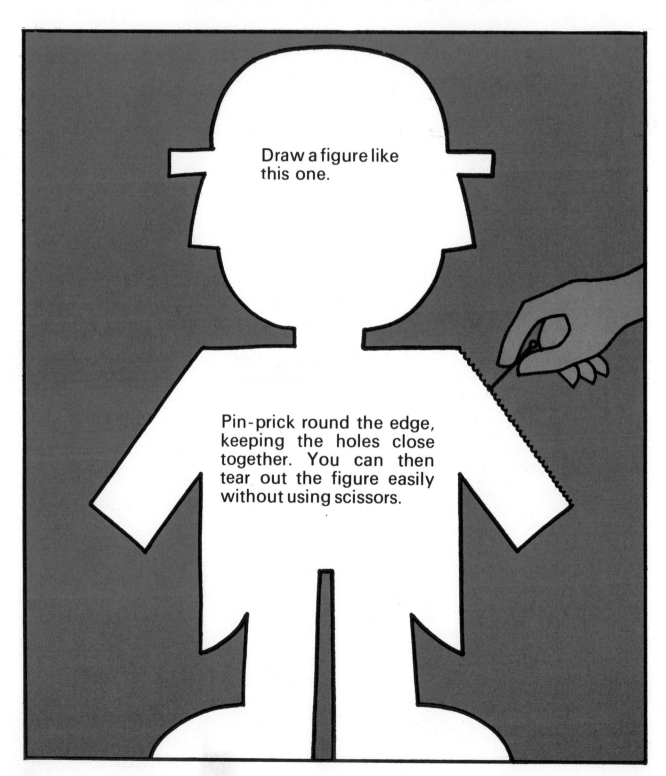

Draw a figure like this one.

Pin-prick round the edge, keeping the holes close together. You can then tear out the figure easily without using scissors.

Fill in with coloured pencils as shown.

PAPER FISH

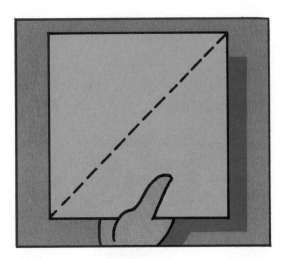

Square a piece of paper. Fold it and cut on the dotted line.

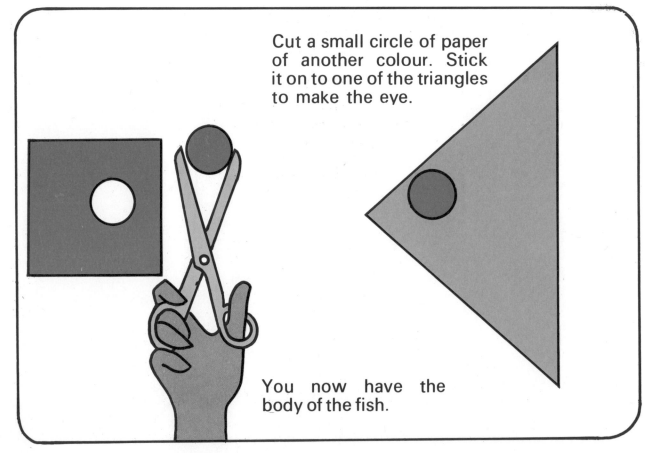

Cut a small circle of paper of another colour. Stick it on to one of the triangles to make the eye.

You now have the body of the fish.

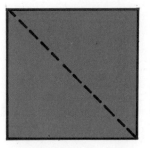

Now make the tail. Cut another, smaller, triangle in a different colour from the body.

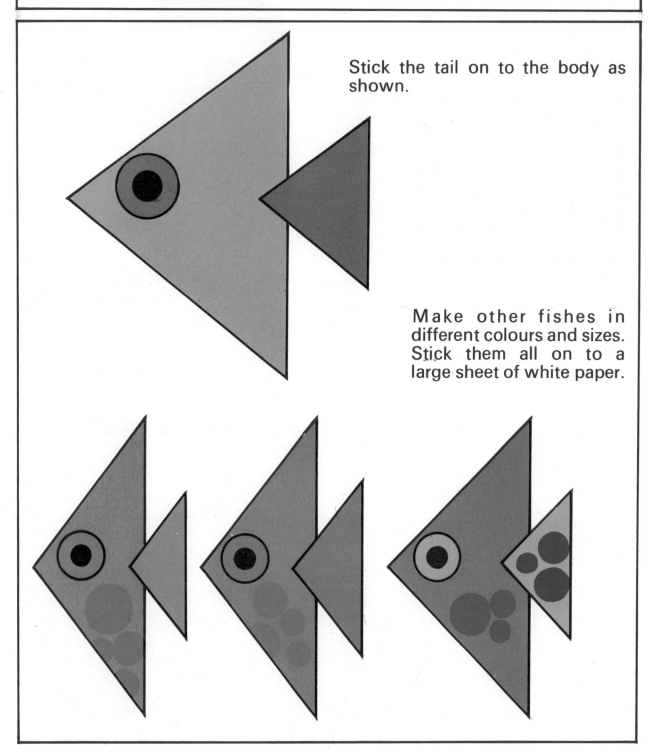

Stick the tail on to the body as shown.

Make other fishes in different colours and sizes. Stick them all on to a large sheet of white paper.

CUTTING OUT AND STICKING SHAPES

Cut shapes like these out of shiny coloured paper.

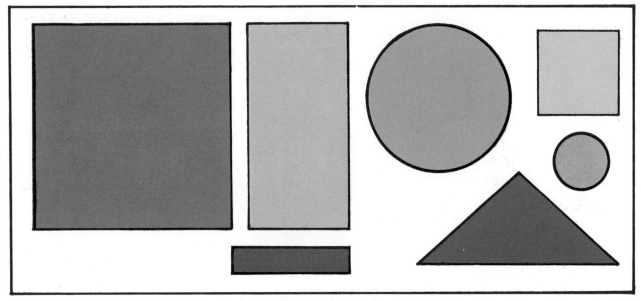

Stick the shapes on to a sheet of white or coloured paper as shown in the pictures.

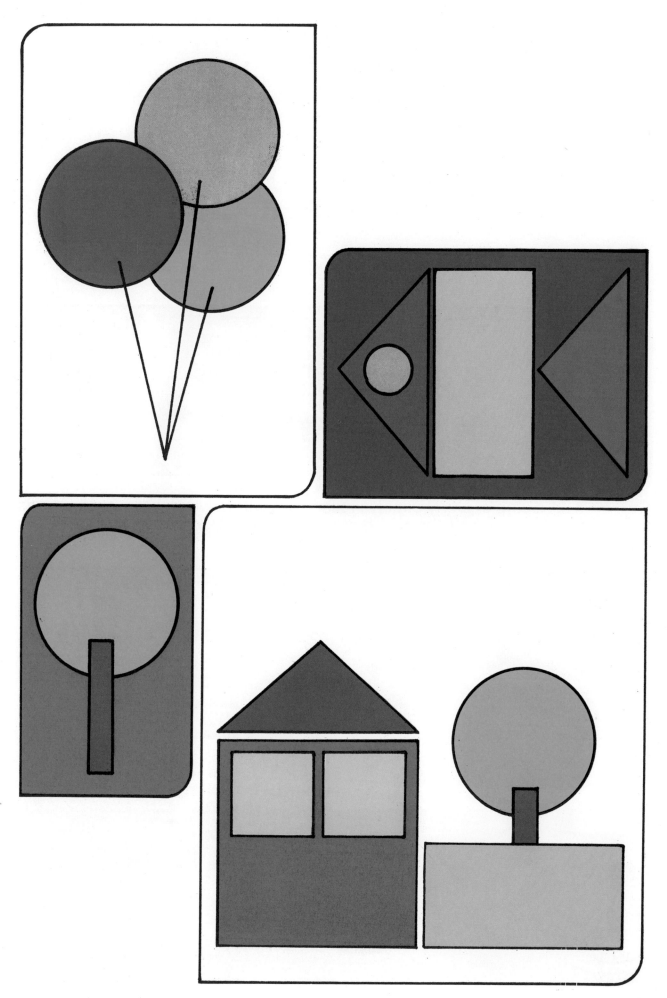

MATERIALS:
● Shiny
  paper
● Scissors
● Ruler
● Pencil

MORE PAPER CHAINS

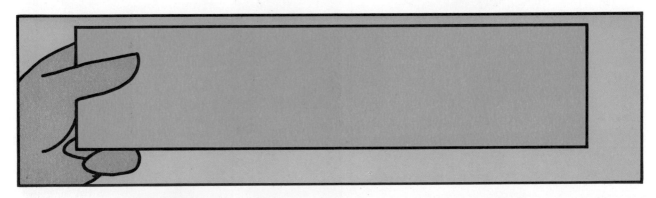

Cut out a long strip of shiny paper. Measure its width. Make as many divisions as you can equal to half the width along the strip. Use a ruler and pencil to mark these divisions.

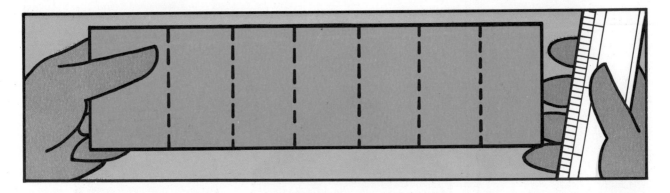

Fold the paper on these lines as shown below.

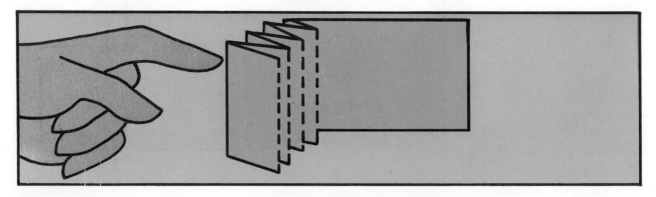

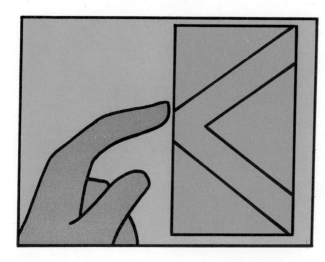

Draw this pattern on the folded paper and cut it out.

Unfold the paper. Now you have a paper chain like this one.

Here is another pattern which you can make in the same way.

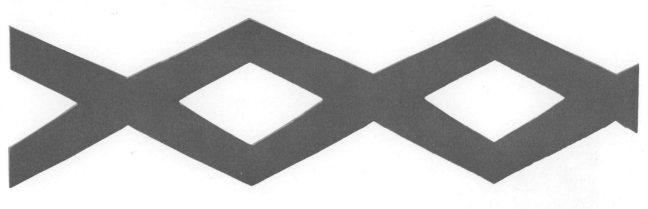

MATERIALS:
- Colour magazines
- Scissors
- Glue
- Shiny coloured paper

SCRAPBOOK

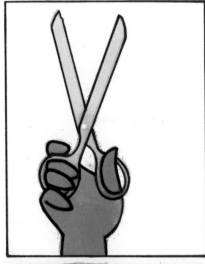

To make up a scrapbook, first get some old colour magazines.

Choose something you like. Cut it out carefully.
Stick the pictures on to a sheet of paper or cardboard. They will look
better if you overlap them slightly and don't arrange them in a straight
line.

MATERIALS:

● Tracing paper
● Coloured paper
● Pencil
● Scissors
● Glue

FACE WITH DIFFERENT EXPRESSIONS

You can see from these drawings that the eyes and mouth can change the expression.

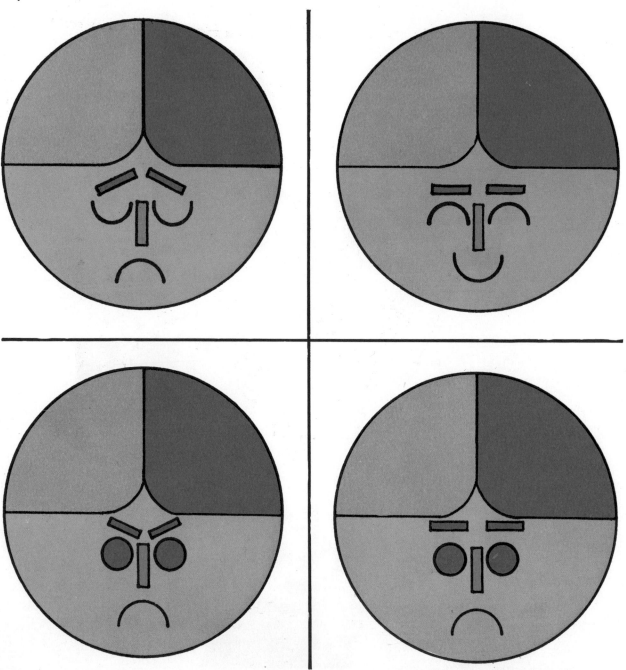

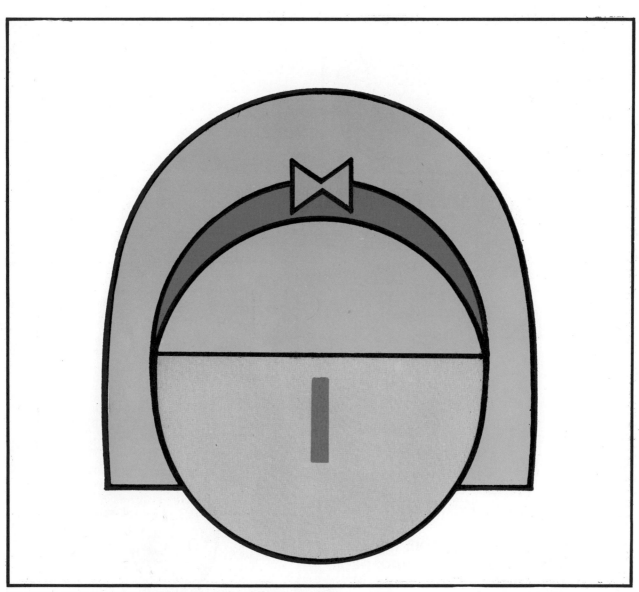

Trace this girl's face. Then cut it out.

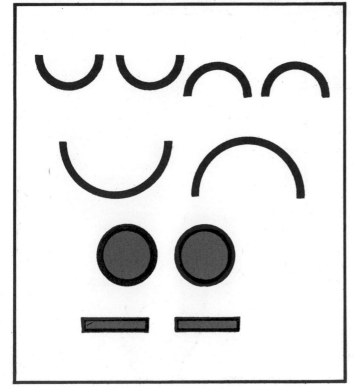

Cut out the different shapes for the eyebrows, eyes and mouth. Now you can make this little girl cry, laugh, smile or look cross.

MATERIALS:

● Paper
● Scissors
● Pin
● Cane or
  thin stick

WINDMILL

Square a piece of paper about the size of a sheet of writing paper. Fold it on the dotted lines. Press hard on the folds so that they stay.

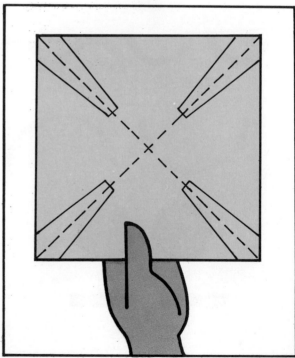

Unfold the paper. Cut along the continuous lines in the corners as shown in the picture.

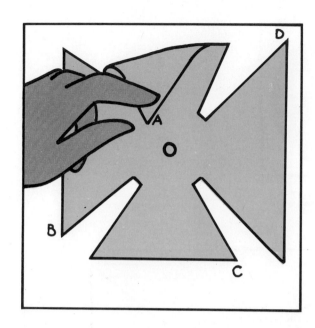

Fold point A over on to point O. Hold it in place. Do the same with points B, C and D.

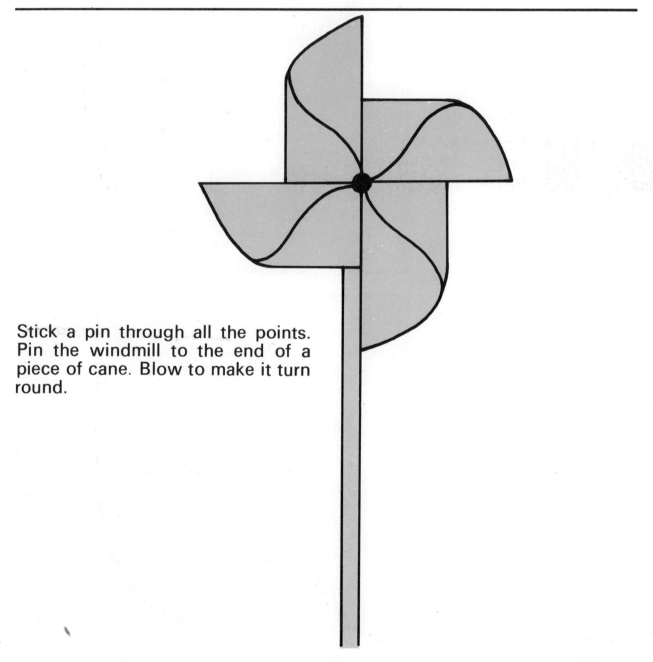

Stick a pin through all the points. Pin the windmill to the end of a piece of cane. Blow to make it turn round.

MASKS

Draw a cat's face on a piece of paper.

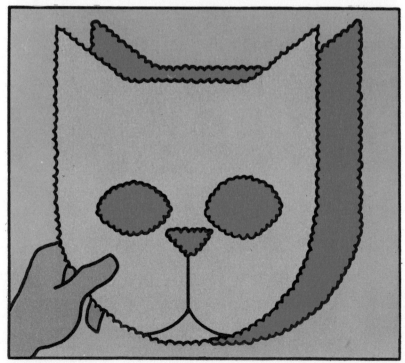

Pin-prick around the drawing so that you can tear it out easily without using scissors.

42

Now you have a mask to make you look like a cat. Draw in the whiskers with a crayon.

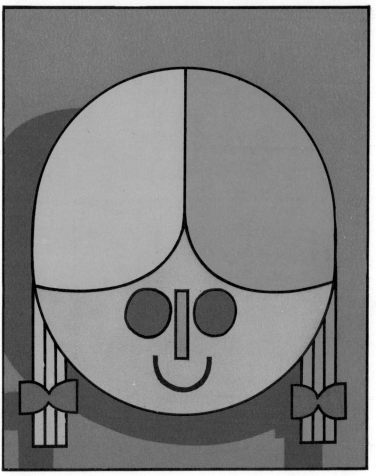

You can make other masks like the one shown on the left.

Hair for a face mask can be made with strips of paper. You can tear the strips or cut them with scissors.

43

COTTAGE

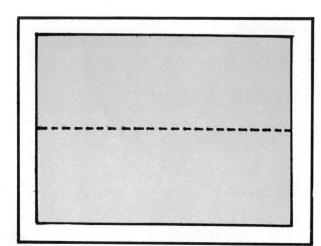

Fold a sheet of paper about 7½in. by 10½in. in half.

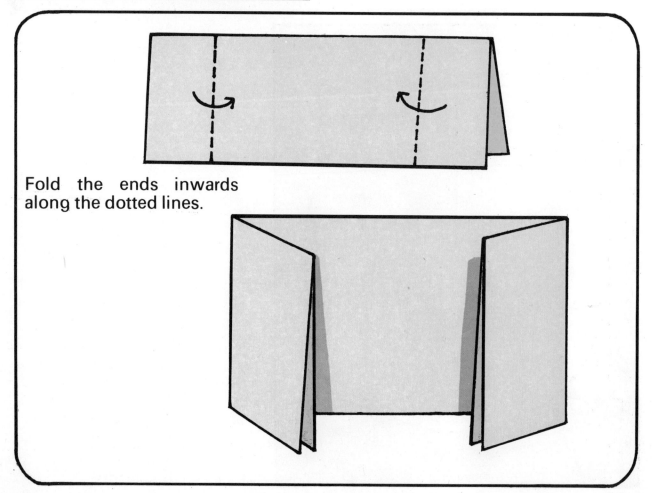

Fold the ends inwards along the dotted lines.

Put your thumb inside the left hand fold as shown in the picture. Open it out and flatten the top.

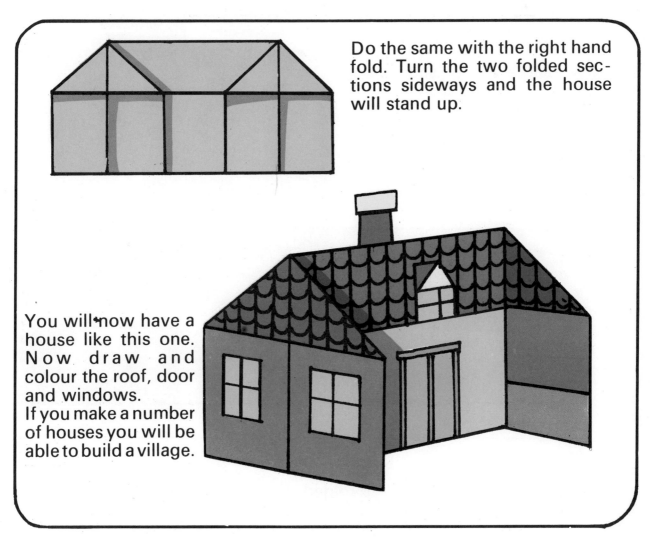

Do the same with the right hand fold. Turn the two folded sections sideways and the house will stand up.

You will now have a house like this one. Now draw and colour the roof, door and windows.
If you make a number of houses you will be able to build a village.

TRAIN

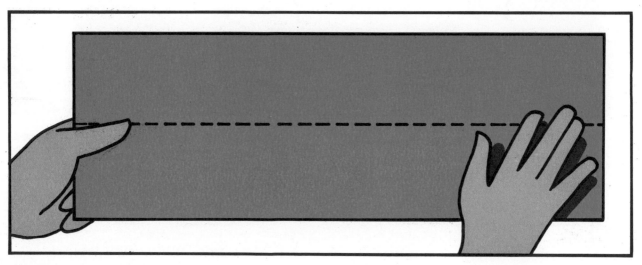

Cut a rectangle out of shiny paper.
Fold along the dotted line.

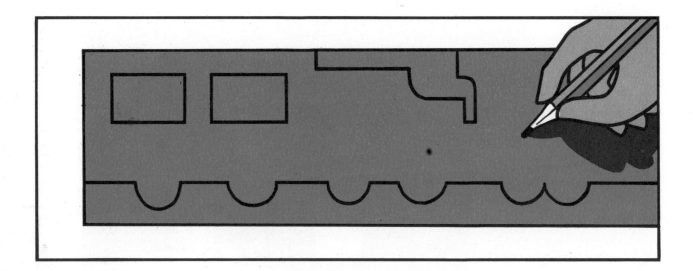

Draw the outline of a train on the folded paper. Try to copy the one in the picture.

Cut it out, following the lines of the drawing.

Unfold the paper and you will be able to stand your train up.

MAKING UP FIGURES

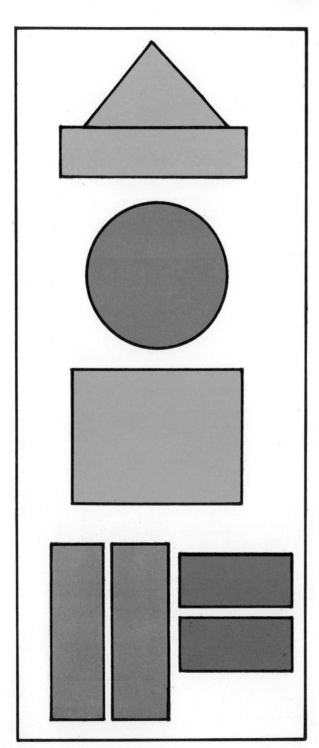

Cut these shapes out of coloured shiny paper.
Stick them on a piece of cardboard as shown opposite.

Now you can make other things. You could use the pieces of paper you have left over, or cut out new shapes.

4

MATERIALS:

- Different coloured shiny paper
- Scissors
- Brush and glue
- White paper

PAPER STRIP LANDSCAPE

Make a drawing like this one on a sheet of white paper.

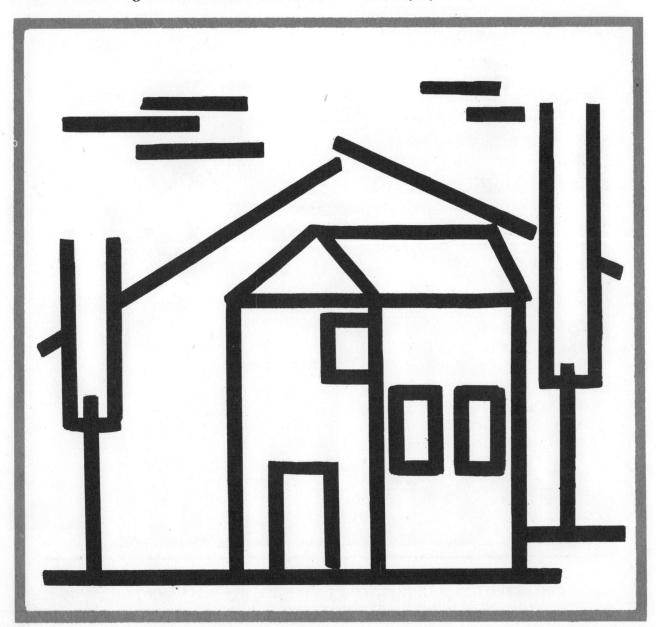

Cut thin strips of shiny paper in blue, brown, green, orange and black.
Stick these strips on the drawing you have made as shown below. You can
make other pictures in the same way.

MOBILE WITH PAPER DISCS

Cut a strip of shiny paper 15in. long. Place a thick pencil at one end and roll the paper round it.

When you get to the end stick down the edge of the paper. Take out the pencil.

You are left with a paper rod.

Cut six discs out of white shiny paper. Cut another six out of blue paper, six out of red paper and six out of black.

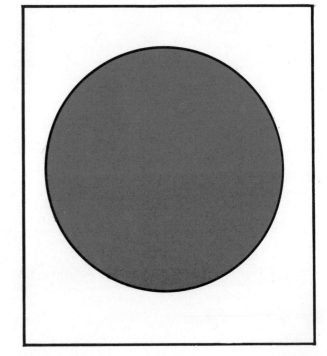

Stick the backs of half the discs on to some pieces of wool.

Stick the other discs on the back of the first ones.

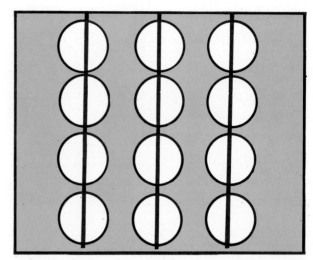

Thread a needle with wool. Pass through the rod.

Make a large knot in the end of each piece.

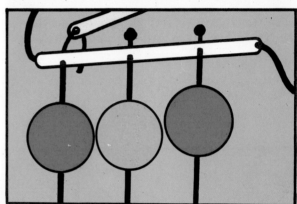

Now you can hang the mobile from the ceiling to decorate your room.

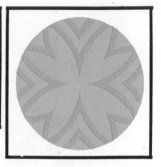

SWALLOW

Cut out a square piece of paper. Fold it to find the diagonal and cut along the fold.

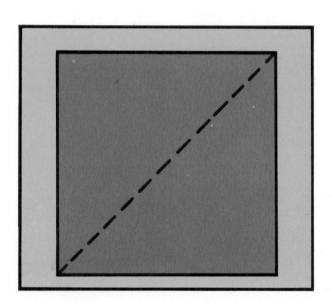

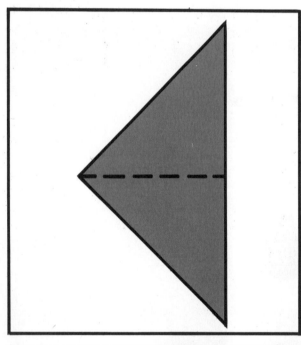

Take one of the triangles and fold along the dotted line.

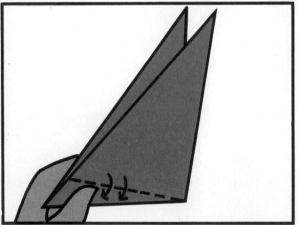

Hold the folded paper between your left thumb and fore-finger. With your right hand, fold the front flap down along the dotted line as shown.

54

Cut two small circles out of paper of another colour. Stick one on either side of the bird's head.

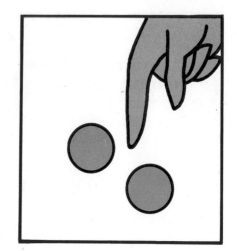

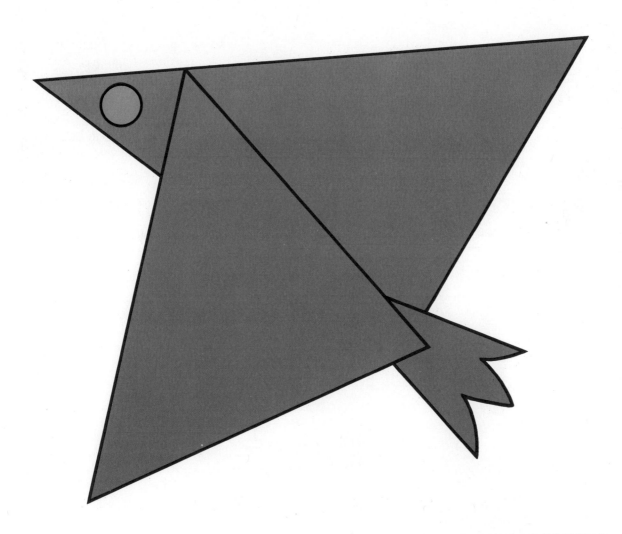

Cut out a tail and stick it in place between the two wings.

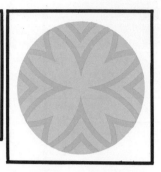

CUT-OUT FIGURES

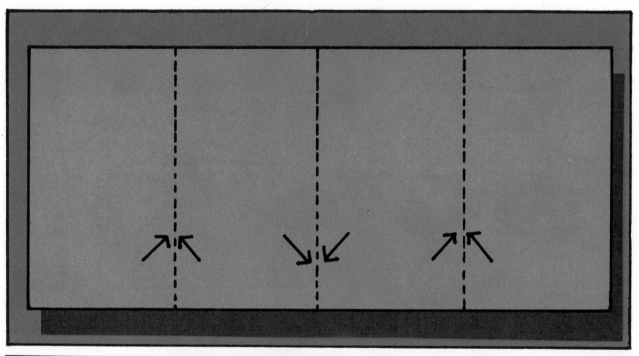

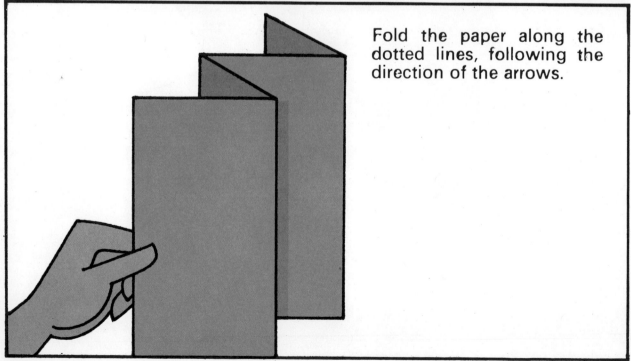

Fold the paper along the dotted lines, following the direction of the arrows.

Draw the outlines shown below on the folded paper.

Cut round the outlines, keeping the paper folded.

Unfold the paper. You now have a chain of complete figures although you only drew two halves.

MATERIALS:

- Blue paper
- White paper
- Scissors
- Glue
- Pencil

CUT-OUT PATTERNS

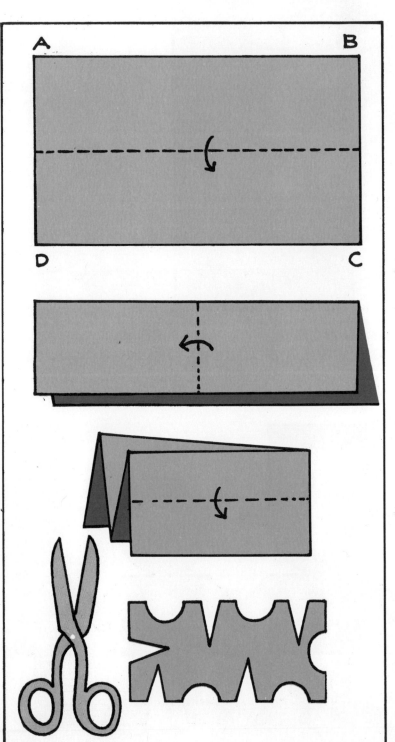

Cut out a rectangle of paper.
Fold it so that A touches D and B touches C.

Fold it twice more along the dotted lines, following the direction of the arrows.

Draw the pattern shown on the left on the folded paper. Then cut it out.

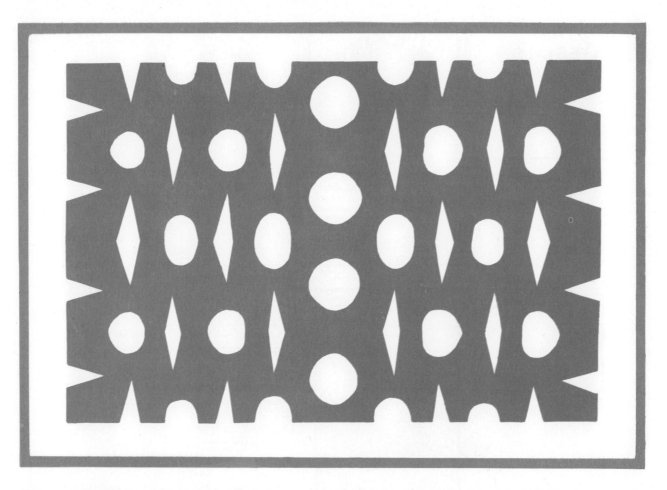

Open out the paper and stick it on to a sheet of white paper with a spot of glue on the corners.

Here are some other patterns you can make.

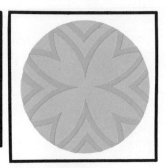

STAR

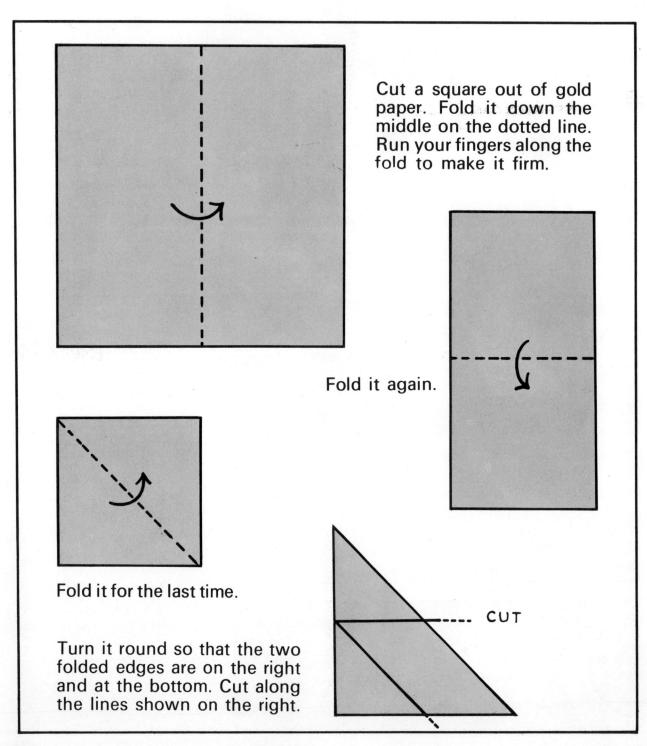

Cut a square out of gold paper. Fold it down the middle on the dotted line. Run your fingers along the fold to make it firm.

Fold it again.

Fold it for the last time.

Turn it round so that the two folded edges are on the right and at the bottom. Cut along the lines shown on the right.

CUT

Open out the paper completely. You will now have a star like this one.

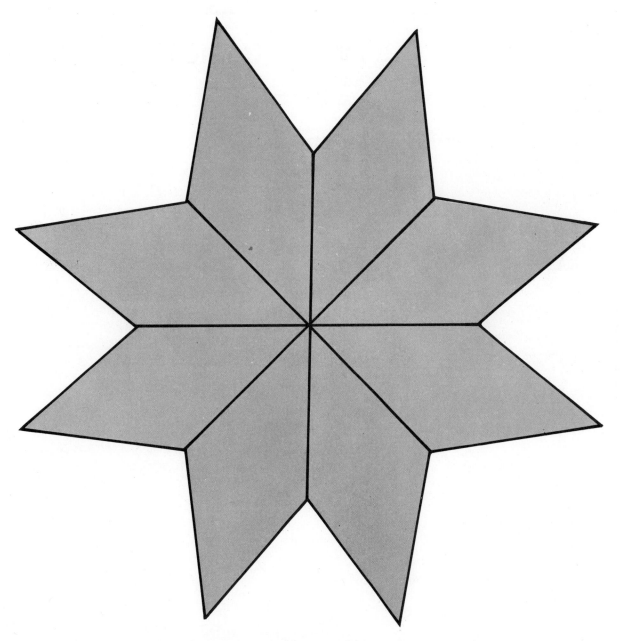

You can make various gold and silver stars in this way, in different sizes. Use the stars as Christmas decorations.

MATERIALS:

- Different coloured paper
- Glue
- Sticky tape
- White paper
- Black paper
- Scissors

WRIGGLING SNAKE

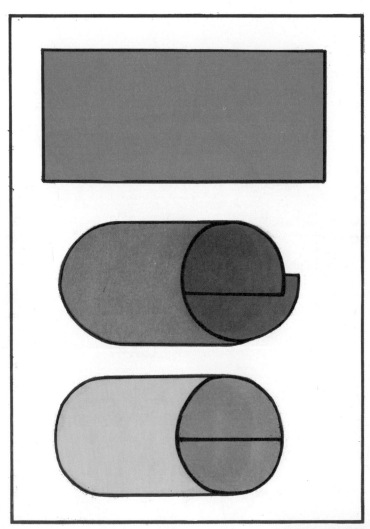

The body of this wriggling snake is made from several rings of the same size but different colours. The rings are made with rectangles of paper about 5in. by 1½in. Glue the short ends together.

The head of the snake is made from a square of paper about 5in. by 5in.

Stick two white circles on the top part of the head, and stick two black ovals in the middle of them.

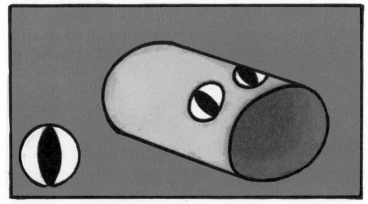

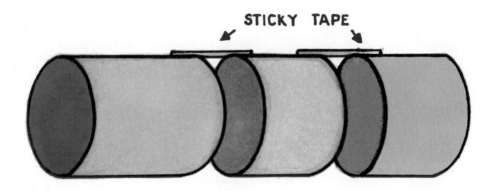

STICKY TAPE

Join each ring to the next at the top with sticky tape. You can also sew the rings together with strong cotton, but this is more difficult.

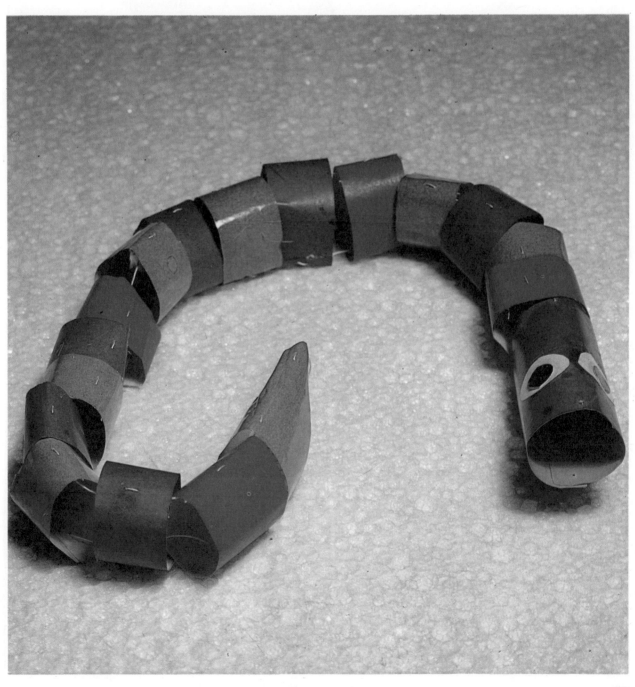

WITCH

This witch is made from pieces of coloured paper. You can use whatever colours you like.

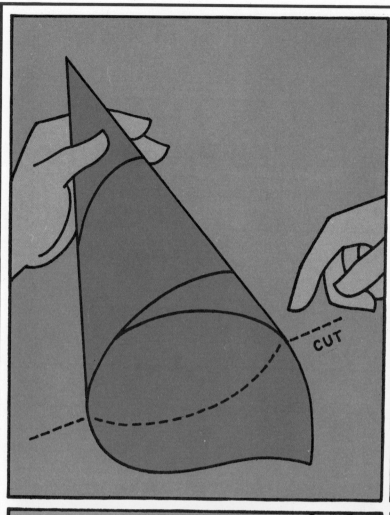

Make a paper cone. Cut the end off so the bottom is level.

Draw the face on a piece of plain paper.

Cut a blue ring for the witch's hat.

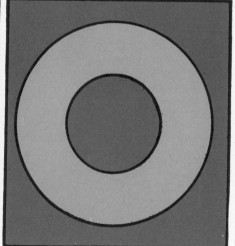

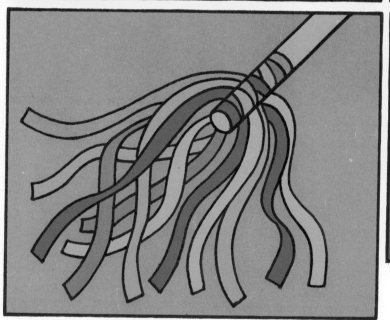

Cut some narrow strips of paper and wind them round the broomstick.

To make the cloak, glue a strip of paper round the neck so the corners meet at the front. Draw in the hands so they stick out from under the cloak.

5

PIRANA FISH

Cut a square out of green paper.
Keep folding it as shown on these pages. Then open it up and fold the corners.
It should now form a small table. Fold the table along one of the diagonal lines
so that point B touches point C, and stick the two halves together.

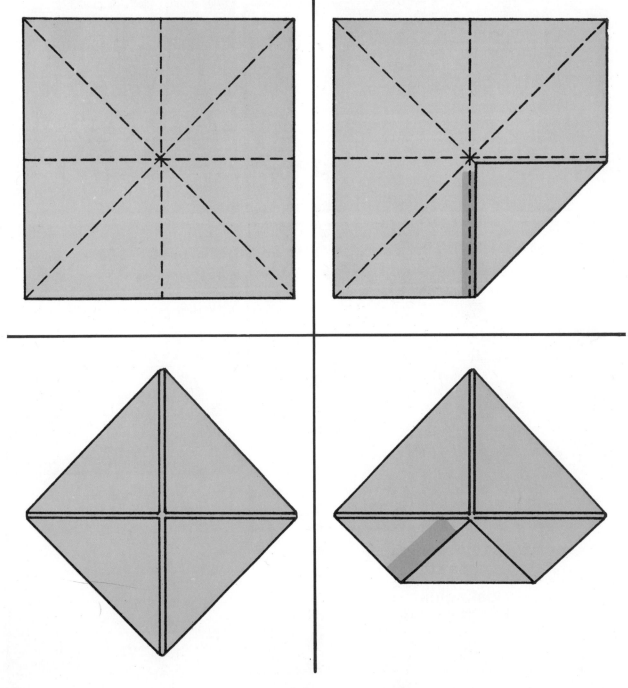

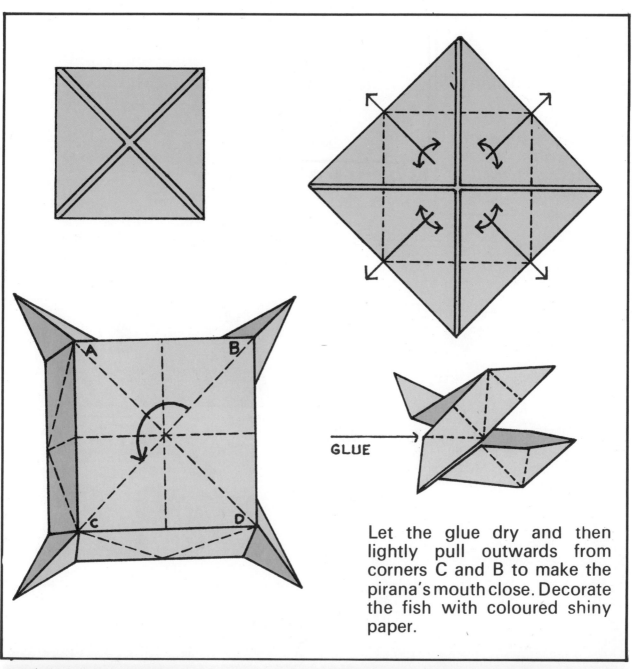

GLUE

Let the glue dry and then lightly pull outwards from corners C and B to make the pirana's mouth close. Decorate the fish with coloured shiny paper.

MATERIALS:

- **Different coloured shiny paper**
- **Scissors**
- **Thin stick or match**
- **Nylon thread**
- **Needle**

NECKLACE

Cut some circles this size out of shiny yellow paper.

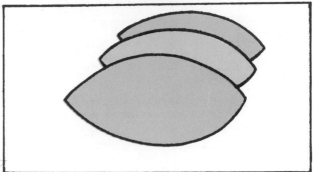

Cut this shape out of shiny green and blue paper.

Roll the blue and green paper round a thin stick. Glue down the end of each and remove the stick to make the small, straight beads.

Make the large beads in the same way, copying the pattern shown below.

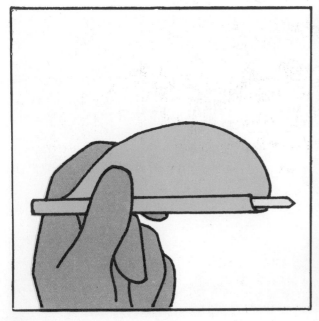

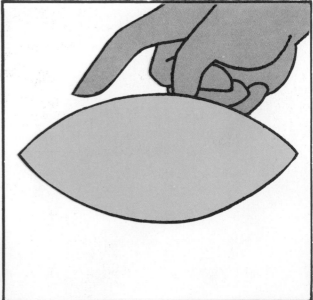

Thread a needle with nylon thread.
Pass it through the hollow centre
of the long beads. Alternate with
the round beads as shown below.

Make a bracelet to go with the
necklace.

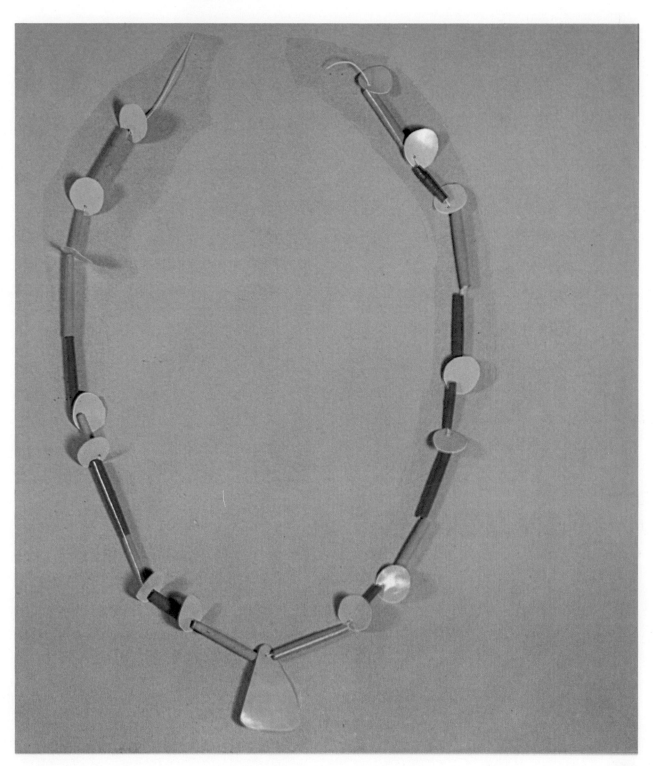

MATERIALS:

● Black paper
● Coloured cellophane
● Pencil
● Scissors
● Glue

STAINED-GLASS WINDOW

Cut two squares the same size out of black paper. Cut a square out of the middle of each and stick the frames together.

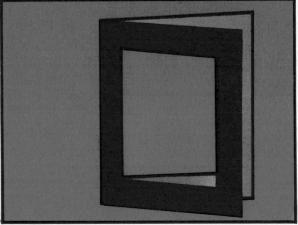

Stick the cellophane over the frame as if it were the glass.

Cut a small house out of the paper you
have left. Now stick it on to the cellophane.

**Another
shape**

MATERIALS:
- Black paper
- White crayon
- Cellophane or shiny paper
- Scissors
- Glue

ANOTHER STAINED-GLASS WINDOW

Cut a square out of black paper. Fold it down the middle.

Draw half a house and cut it out.

Cover the space with red cellophane. Stick it on carefully.

Hold it against a window-pane or in front of a light. It looks like a stained-glass window.

Another shape

Cover the space with orange shiny paper.

PEACOCK

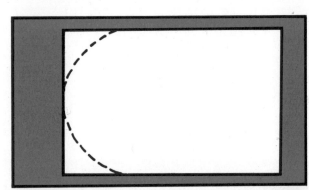

Take a sheet of white paper 10½in. by 15½in. First of all draw the shape shown and cut along the line.

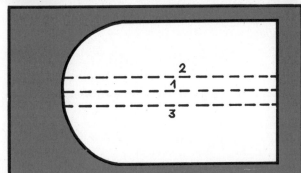

Fold the paper in half along line 1. Then fold it in opposite directions on lines 2 and 3.

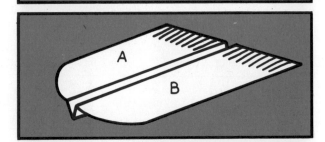

Now cut a fringe along the back edge.

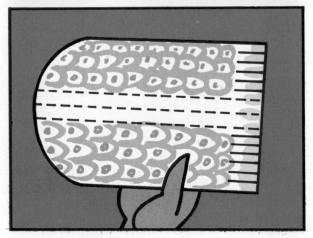

Unfold the paper carefully. Decorate parts A and B with a thick felt-tip pen as shown in the picture.

Next, fold the paper again as you did before. Stick the two sides that are folded inwards together.

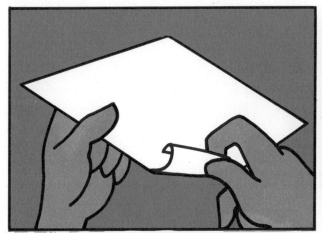

To make the neck and legs, roll up a sheet of white paper 10½ in. by 15½ in., starting at one corner. Cut off two pieces of the tube, each 2½ in. long. These form the legs. The rest is the neck.

The head is a small rectangle of dark blue shiny paper cut as shown above. Stick it on to the top part of the neck. Stick all these parts to the peacock's body.

This peacock was thought up by a child of six. It is very easy to make. You can work out how to make other animals yourself.

DRAGON

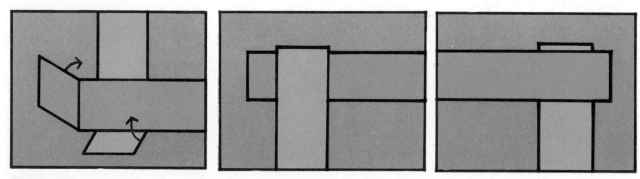

THE BODY:

Cut two strips of green paper about 20in. long, $\frac{1}{2}$in. wide at one end and $1\frac{1}{4}$in. at the other.

Stick the two wide ends together at right angles and fold one over the other as shown above.

THE LEGS:

For each leg cut two strips $\frac{1}{2}$in. wide and much shorter than those you used to make the body, and fold together in the same way.

76

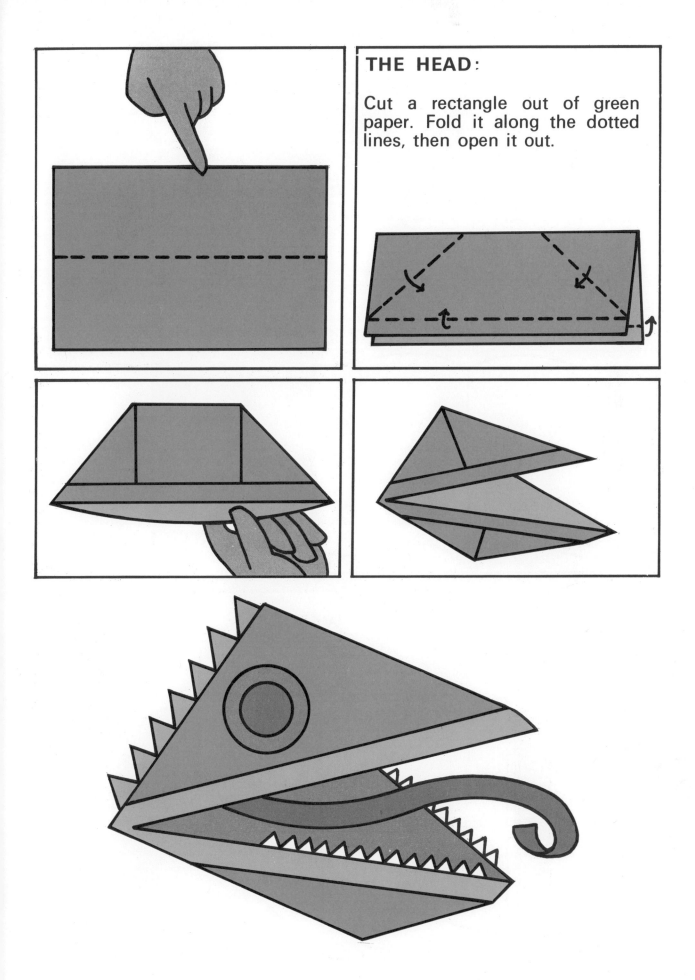

THE HEAD:

Cut a rectangle out of green paper. Fold it along the dotted lines, then open it out.

Add the eyes, tongue, teeth etc cut out of shiny coloured paper.

COVERING BOOKS

Here are two simple ways of covering books to keep them clean.

FIRST WAY

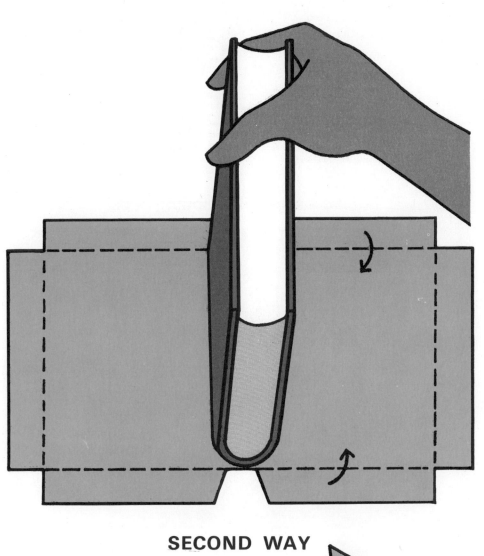

SECOND WAY

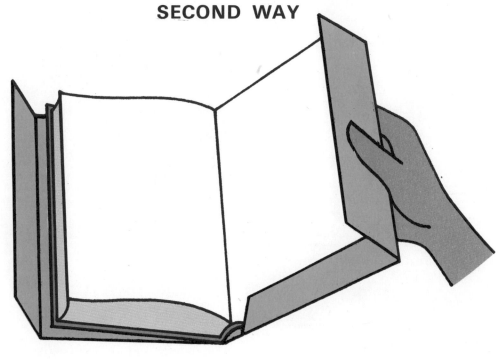

MATERIALS:

- Wrapping paper
- Pencil
- Scissors
- Glue

CUT-OUTS

Square a sheet of wrapping paper.

Fold it as shown.

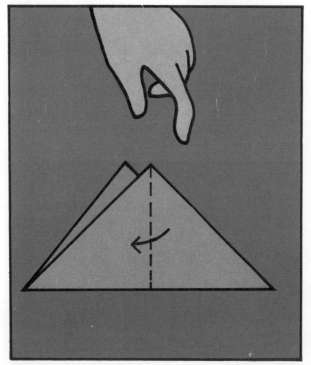

Draw the pattern and cut it out.

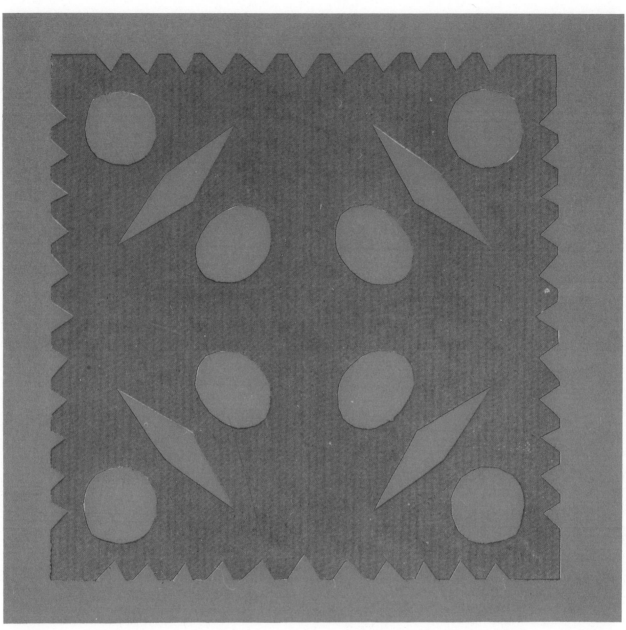

Open out the paper. Stick it on to another sheet.

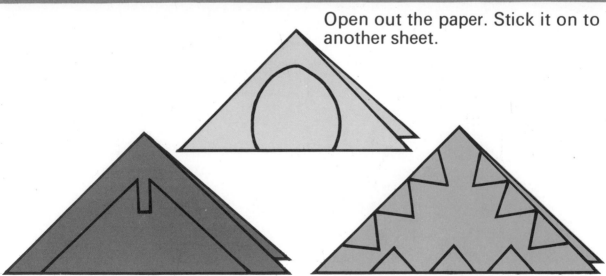

Make other patterns in the same way.

MOBILE

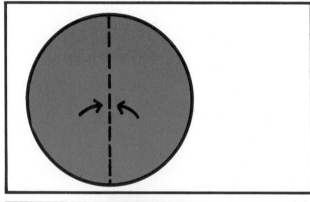

Cut four discs about 7½in. in diameter out of red paper.

Fold them down the middle.

Open them a little.

Join the four discs at the folds. Stick one half of each disc to one half of the next one. Stick them together round a piece of wool as shown.

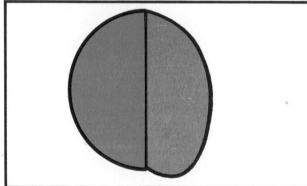

Cut three 5in. squares out of blue paper.
Fold them as shown below. Stick one half of one square to half of the next, round the wool that passes through the discs.

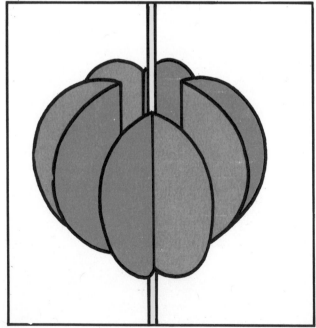

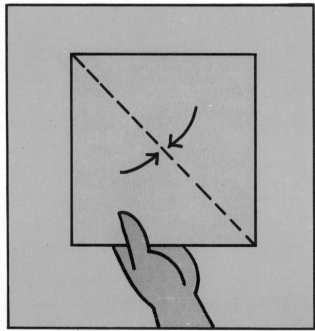

Cut four discs 4in. in diameter out of green paper, and three 3½in. squares out of black paper.
Make up in the same way as the other circles and squares.

You now have a mobile. Fix the end of the length of wool to the ceiling with a drawing pin.

RABBIT

THE HEAD:

Cut a rectangle 9in. by 2½in.
Cut a circle out of it 1¾in. in diameter.
Stick the ends of the rectangle together to make a cylinder.

THE BODY:

Cut another rectangle 7in. by 6in.
Stick the ends together.

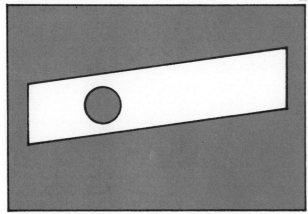

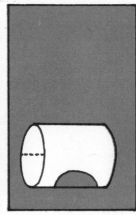

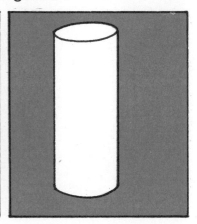

THE BASE:

Cut a rectangle 11in. by 2½in.
Cut out of it a circle 1¾in. in diameter.
Fold under on the dotted lines and stick the flaps together.

WHISKERS:

Use narrow strips of different coloured shiny paper.

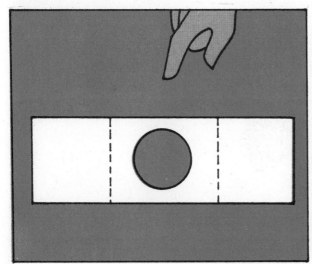

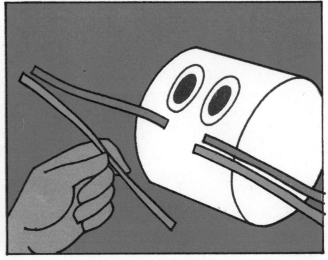

Decorate the rabbit with thick felt-tip pens.

SEAL

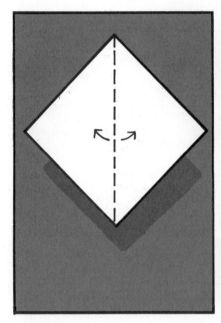

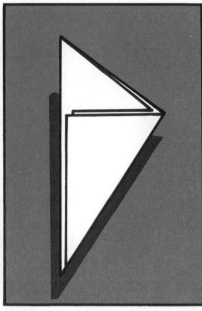

Cut a square of paper. Fold the paper along the dotted line. Now fold over the bottom right hand side, then the top right hand side. Open the paper out and make a fold at the middle of the sides as shown. Cut a slit in the end of the fold that runs along the top of the tail.

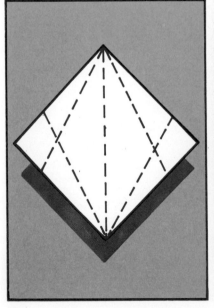

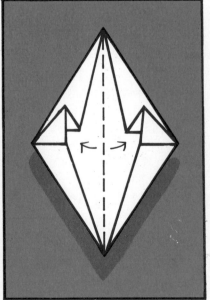

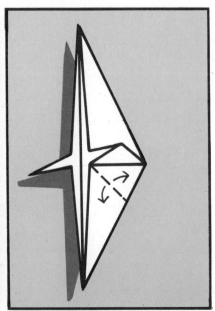

86

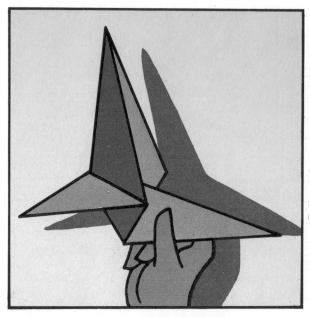

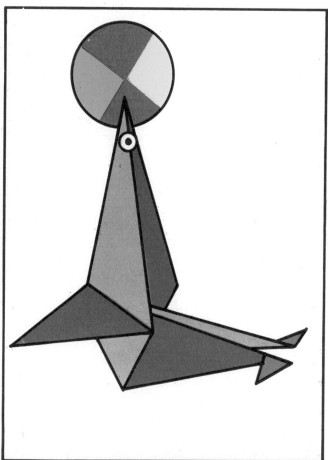

The eyes are two discs in a different colour. Make a cut in the top of the face to make the mouth. Slot the ball, which is a circle of different coloured paper, into the mouth.

MATERIALS:

- Stiff paper or card
- Colour magazines
- White paper
- Different coloured shiny paper
- Scissors
- Glue

CIRCUS RING

THE FOUR POLES:

Use white paper to make the poles. Roll each piece of paper into a rod. Make four cuts at the bottom. Fold the flaps out. Wrap strips of shiny red paper round the pole.

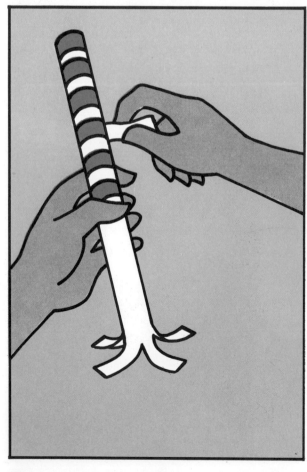

THE GROUND:

Cut a cardboard rectangle 10½in. by 15½in. Stick the poles on to it.

THE BARRIERS:

Cut two strips of shiny paper 10in. by 1in. Decorate them with rectangles of paper in a different colour.

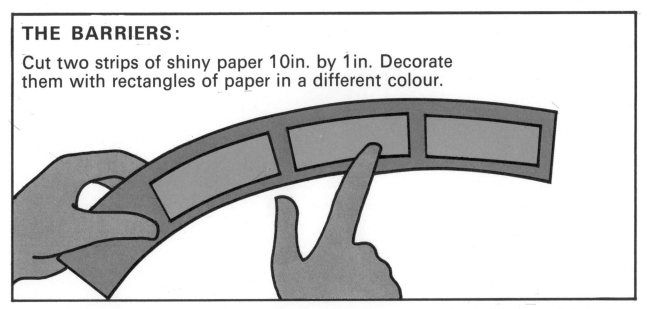

To keep the barriers upright, cut several small rectangles of paper. Stick three of them to each barrier as supports.
Put the seals you have made inside the ring.
Cut any other circus animals you find out of magazines.

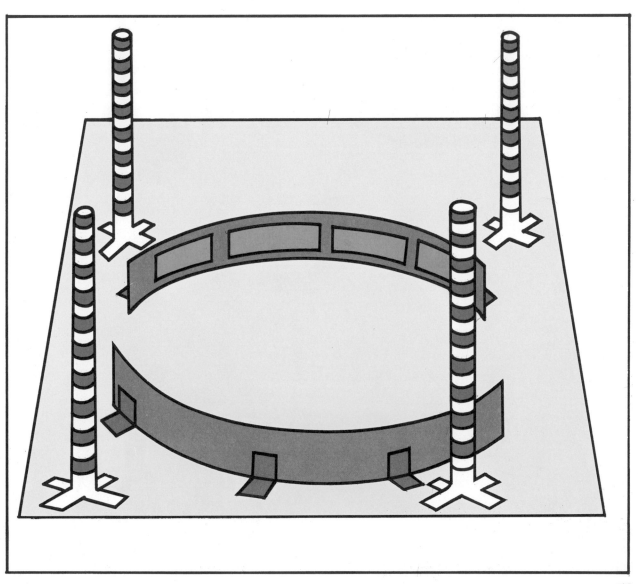

NECKLACE

Cut this shape out of different coloured papers.

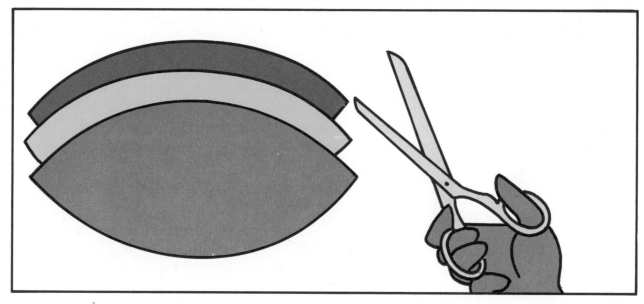

Roll each piece of paper round a thin stick as shown.

Glue down the outside tip of paper with a spot of glue and pull out the stick. Thread all the beads on to a piece of nylon thread.

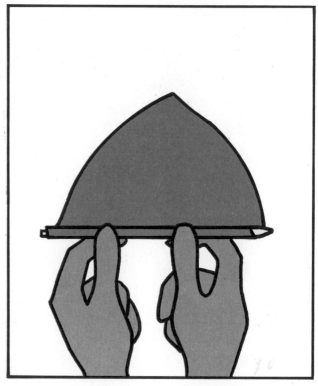

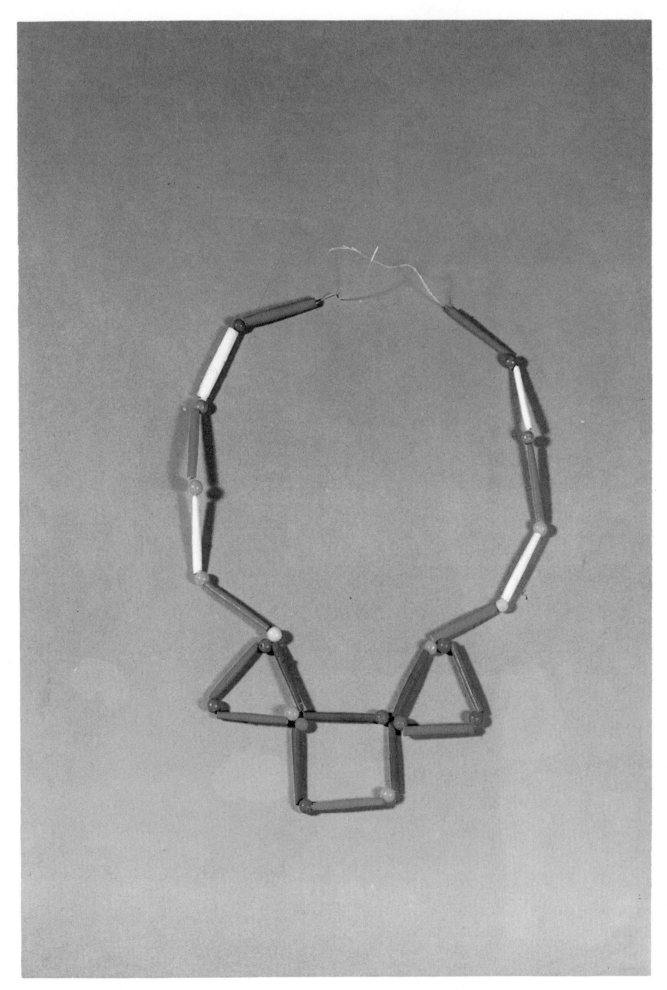

MATERIALS:

- ● **Green and yellow tissue paper**
- ● **Scissors**
- ● **Glue**
- ● **Brush**
- ● **White paper**

CUT-OUT PATTERNS

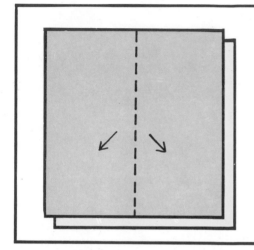

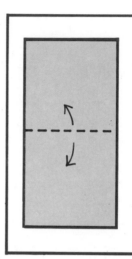

Fold them twice more as shown.

Place one sheet of tissue paper on top of another. Fold them both on the dotted line.

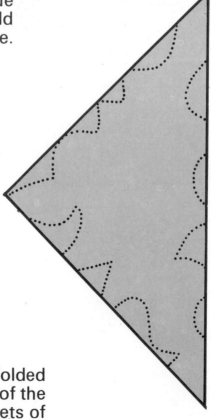

Cut round the edge of the folded paper, following the pattern of the dotted lines. Unfold the sheets of paper.

Stick the cut-out patterns to a sheet of white paper as shown.

WALL DECORATION

Cut a fairly long rectangle of paper.
Fold it on the dotted line.
Cut the folded paper along the continuous lines as shown below.

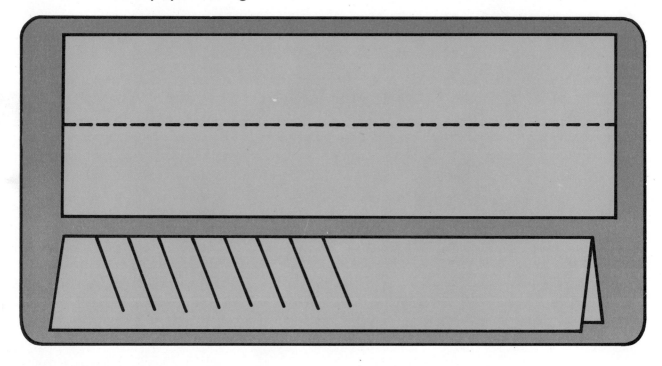

Unfold the paper.
Fold every other cut sideways on the dotted lines.

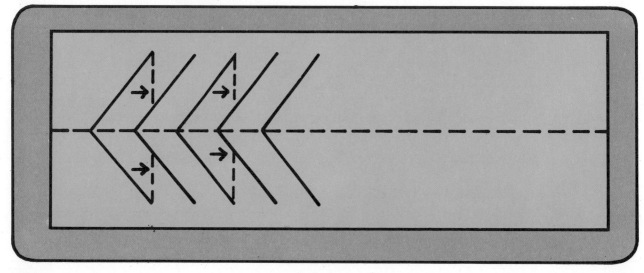

94

95

LION

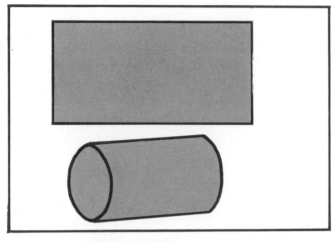

Cut a rectangle of paper out of a colour magazine. Glue two sides together to make a tube.

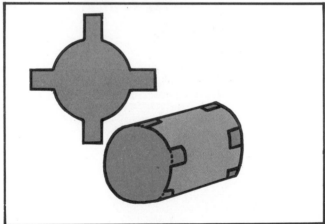

To cover the open ends of the tube, cut out two circles, each with four tabs. Stick these on to the lion's body.

The legs are four small tubes. Make holes in the body and push the legs in.

Cut very thin strips out of shiny brown paper for the mane.

Cut out and stick on the tail. Then draw in the lion's face with coloured felt-tip pens.

7

SAILING BOAT

Cut a rectangle of paper. Fold it on the dotted lines, following the direction of the arrows, to make the base of the boat.

The poles are tubes. These are made by rolling up rectangles of paper from one of the corners. Make a cut at one end of three poles. Glue the split ends of the poles round the longest one, which is the mast.

Stick on the sails and flag.

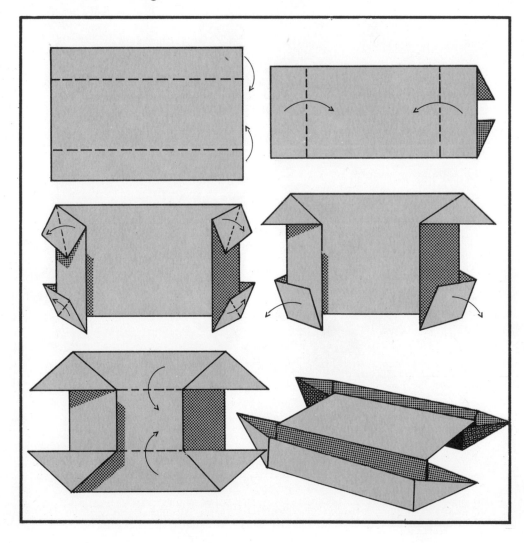

CHRISTMAS DECORATIONS

Cut a square out of coloured cellophane.
Fold it on the dotted lines, following the direction of the arrows. Cut along the continuous line.

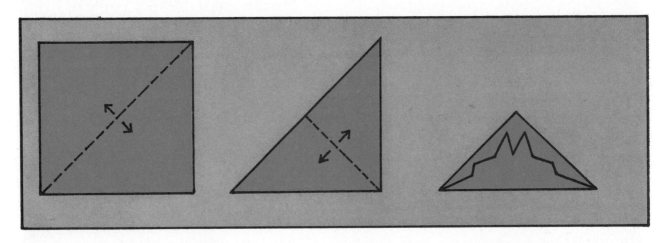

Stick the pattern you have made in the centre of a square of clear cellophane. Stick a blue circle of cellophane on top of it.

Now frame your work with silver paper. Then you can stick it up on your window.

You can make other patterns as well.

COCKATOO

Cut a square out of green paper. Fold it across the middle (fig 1). Fold the corners so that they touch the middle fold (fig 2 and 3). Unfold it to make a new square (fig 4). Fold it down the middle with the corners of the paper on the inside. Then, turn the new corners down on to the new fold (fig 5). Now you have to make the shape in fig 6. Unfold it and you will be left with the square in fig 7. To make the cockatoo all you need to do is to fold the square diagonally, and pull out with your finger those corners which do not lie on the fold.

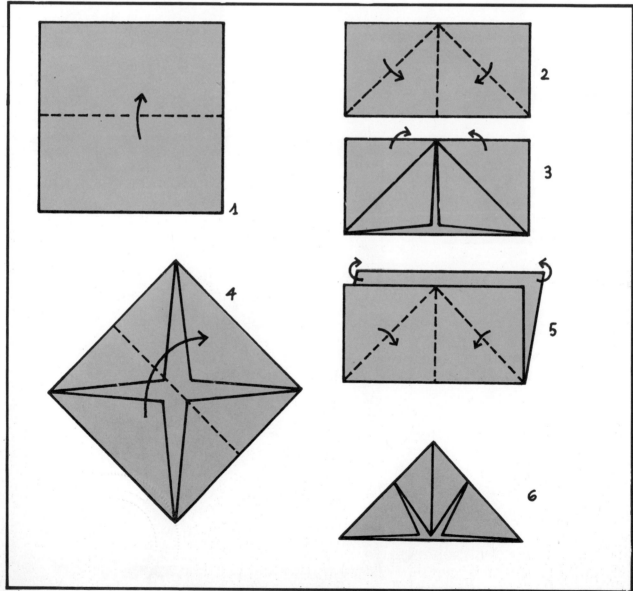

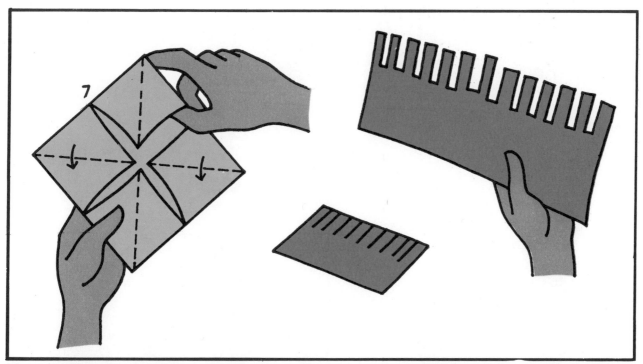

Now make the feathers with strips of coloured paper. Cut fringes and curl up the ends.

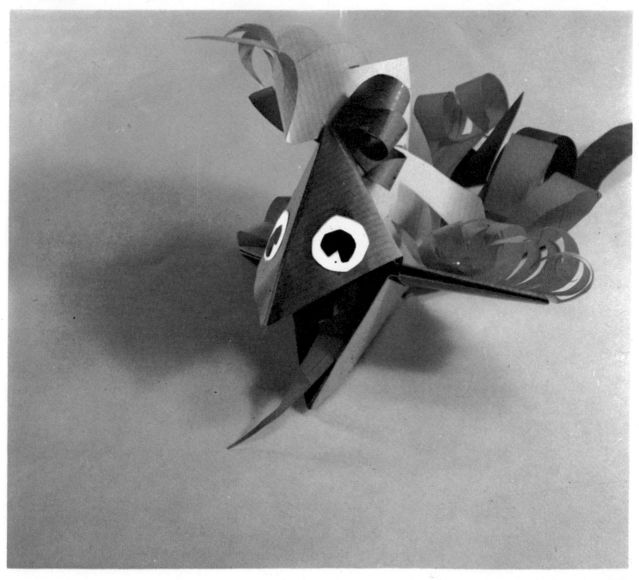

CUT-OUT MOBILE

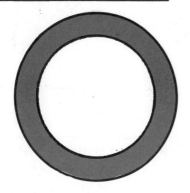

Cut six rings of card.

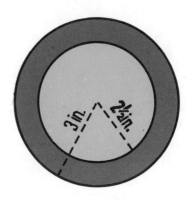

Cut six circles of cellophane.

Cut six pieces of tissue paper, each 4½in. square. Fold them as shown.

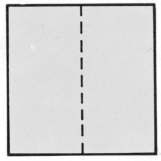 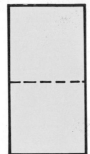

You will end up with six triangles.

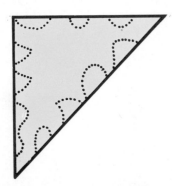

Cut the pattern shown by the dotted lines above out of each triangle. Open them out.

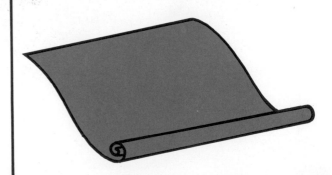

Make a rod from a piece of shiny paper 8in. long.

104

Take one of the rings and place on it in this order:

—a short piece of wool
—a cellophane circle
—a cut-out
—another cut-out
—another cellophane circle
—another ring.

Stick these materials together. Do this twice more.

MATERIALS:
● White
  paper
● Scissors
● Glue
● Felt-tip
  pens

ELEPHANT

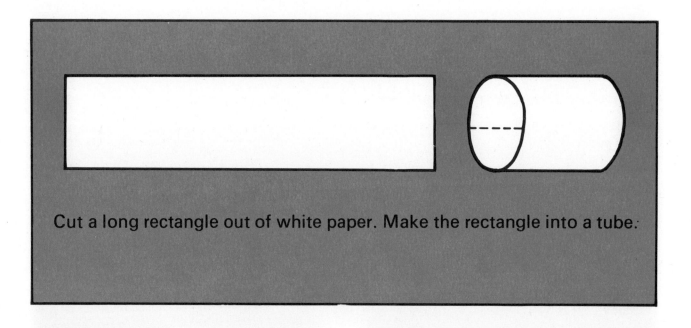

Cut a long rectangle out of white paper. Make the rectangle into a tube.

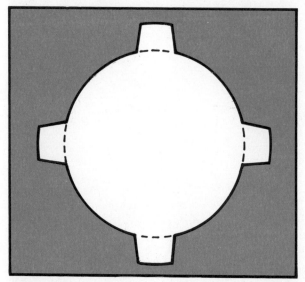

Cut two circles like this with tabs on to cover the open ends of the tube.

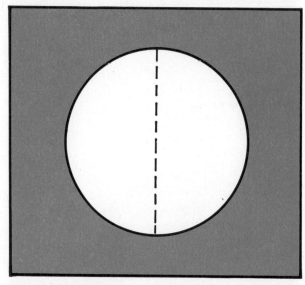

Cut out another circle and halve it for the ears.

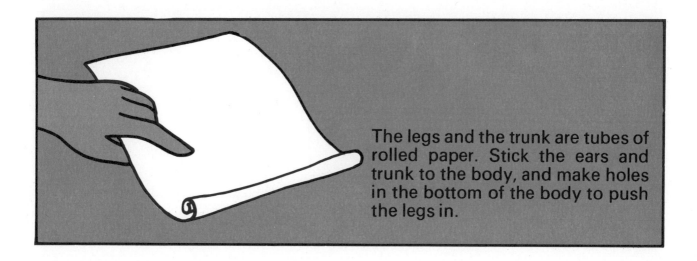

The legs and the trunk are tubes of rolled paper. Stick the ears and trunk to the body, and make holes in the bottom of the body to push the legs in.

Decorate the elephant with coloured felt-tip pens as shown below. You can make other animals in the same way.

COCK

Trace this pattern for the cock's body.
Make the feathers with strips of different coloured tissue paper.

The feathers are stuck on the tail. Cut out the other shapes for the eye, feet, etc. and stick on the body.

Pin the finished bird on the wall. The feathers will move in the slightest breeze and make the cock more lifelike.

VASE OF FLOWERS

Cut two circles out of blue paper. Stick them together, back to back.

Cut out a slightly smaller yellow circle. Stick it on to the blue one. Cut a zig-zag round the edge of the large circle. Cut out a small blue circle and stick it in the centre.

Make the other flowers in the same way, using different sizes and colours, as shown in the photograph.

Roll rectangles of white paper round a knitting needle as shown to make stalks. Glue them to the backs of the flowers.

Cut a rectangle 5in. by 7½in. out of black paper. Make a flattened tube as shown. Cut a zig-zag at one end and fold the points inwards.

Stick these zig-zags on to a circle 3½in. in diameter to finish the vase.

MATERIALS:
- Orange and green paper
- ruler
- Pencil
- Scissors
- Glue and brush
- White card

PAPER WEAVING

Cut a rectangle out of orange paper.

With a pencil and ruler draw the vertical dividing lines shown below. Cut the paper along the continuous lines. Stick it on to a piece of white card with a spot of glue at A and B.

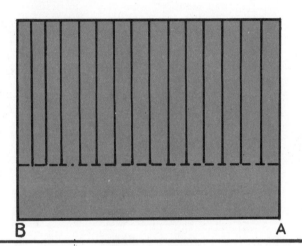

Cut another rectangle out of green paper.

Cut horizontal strips the same width as those on the orange sheet.

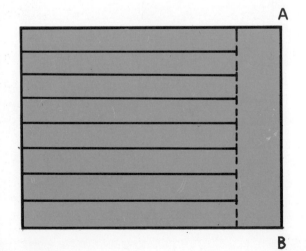

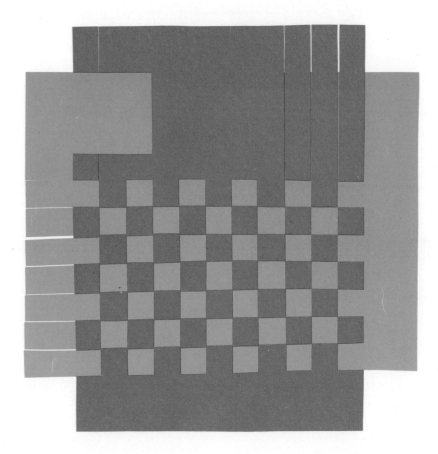

Place this green sheet of paper on the orange one. Weave the strips as shown above. Cut strips of green paper and stick them on to make a frame as shown below.

MATERIALS:
● Different
  coloured paper
● White
  cardboard
● Scissors
● Glue
● Pencil

FRIEZE

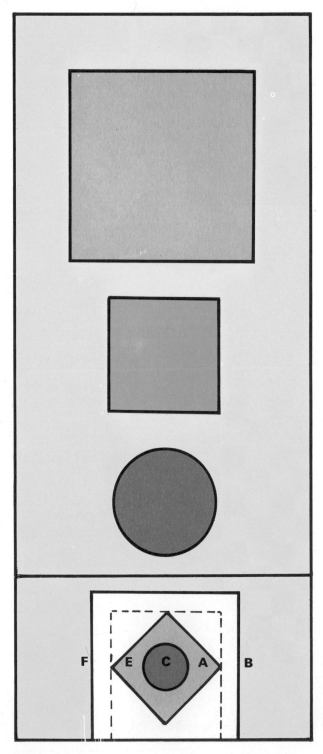

Cut some 3in. squares out of blue paper.

Cut some 2in. squares out of green paper.

Cut out some red circles and stick them in the middle of the blue squares.

Place the first square on a piece of white card. The distance from A to B should be the same as from E to F, and then point C will be the middle of the white card. Continue by putting the other shapes between the two dotted lines.

114

Think up other combinations, using different colours and sizes.

You can use these strips to decorate parcels, book covers and so on.

MATERIALS :

● White card
● Different coloured paper
● Scissors
● Glue

ROCKET

Take a sheet of white paper and make a cone. Stick down the outer edge and level off the bottom.

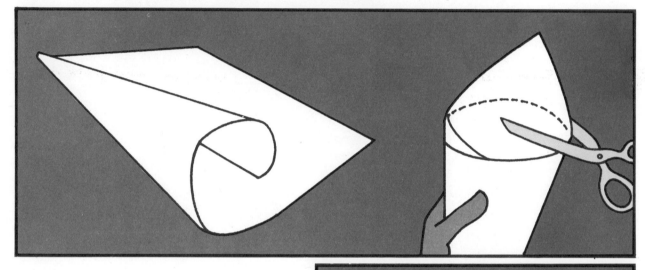

Cut four slots. Make sure they are all the same distance apart.

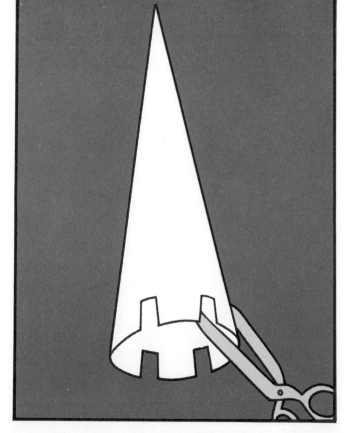

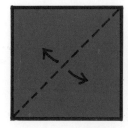   

Square a sheet of coloured paper and fold it as shown.

Open out the paper and use the folds to make the shape shown on the right. Fold the parts together following the arrows. Cut the folded paper on the dotted line.

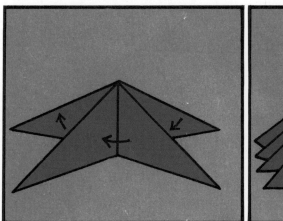 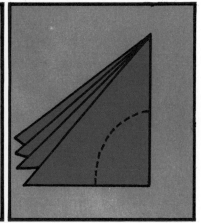

This is the base for the rocket to stand on.

Now you can decorate it with coloured pencils or strips of coloured paper.

JAPANESE LANTERN

Cut four sheets of paper 10½in. by 15½in.

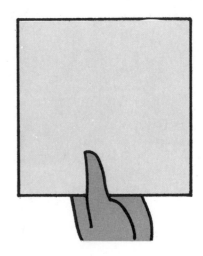

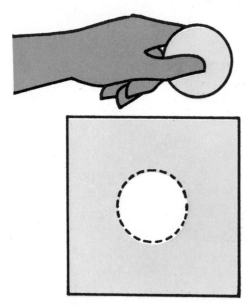

Fold them as shown by the arrows, about ½in. from either end.

Cut two squares 10½in. by 10½in. for the top and bottom.

Cut a circle out of the top square.

Stick the sides to the two squares.

To decorate the lantern first stick a circle of red paper in the middle of two opposite sides.

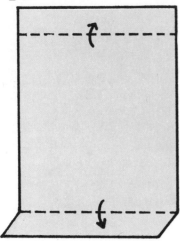

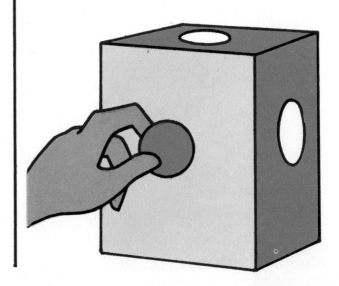

Cover the other two sides with red paper with a circle cut out of the middle. Cover the top and bottom with red paper as well. Hang the lantern from the ceiling with very thin wire.

COVERING BOOKS

Here is a good way to cover books to keep them clean.

Place the book on a sheet of paper, leaving wide margins on the four sides. Then cut on the dotted lines.

Fold the middle strips at the top and bottom inwards under the book.

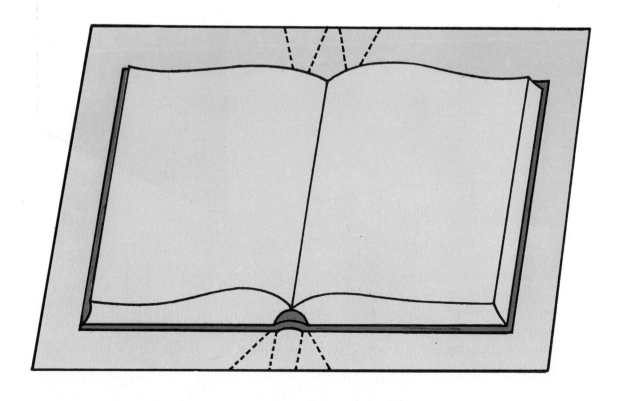

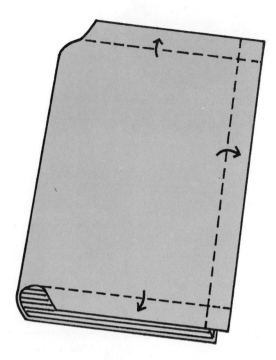

Close the book and fold the
paper as shown.

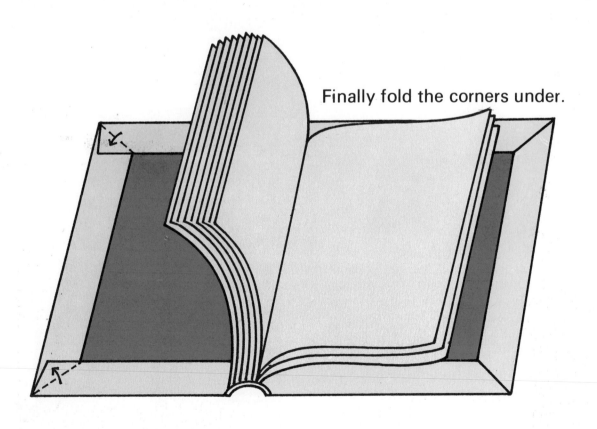

Finally fold the corners under.

TUBULAR MOBILE

Cut a strip of white paper.

Cut about nine rectangles 7½in. wide and of different lengths out of coloured paper. Make each one 1½in. longer than the last, the shortest one being about 11½in. long.

Roll each rectangle round a stick to make tubes.

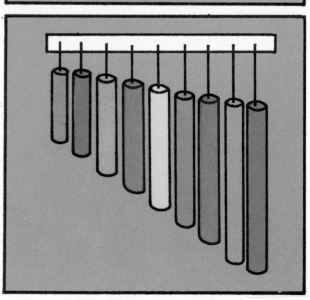

Place the white strip horizontally. Place the first tube vertically a little way below it. Place each tube a little farther away from the horizontal strip. Take a length of cotton and glue one end inside the first tube. Glue the other end on to the white strip. Do the same with the other tubes.

You now have a decorative mobile which looks like a musical instrument.

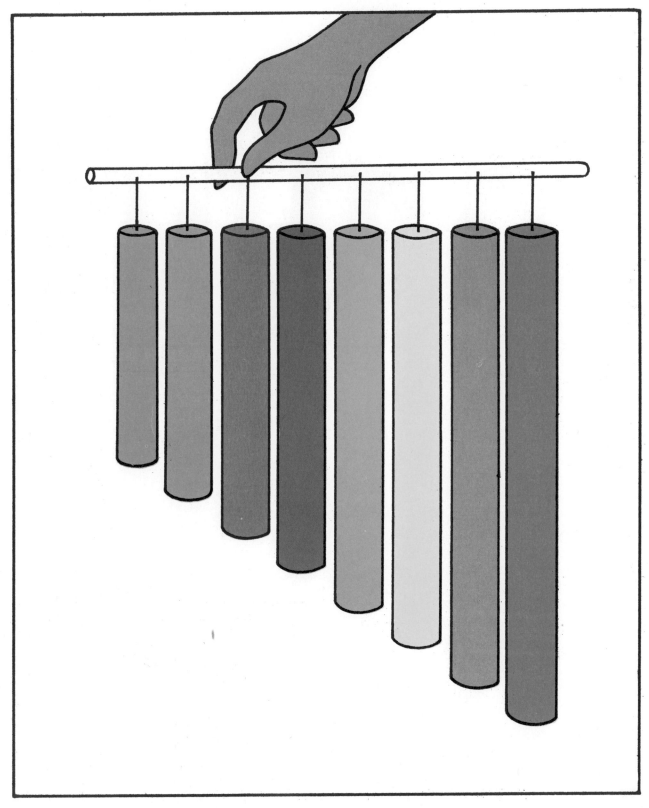

OWL

THE BODY OF THE OWL

Cut a rectangle out of white paper and make it into a cylinder. Cut wings like those below out of brown paper. Stick them to the body.

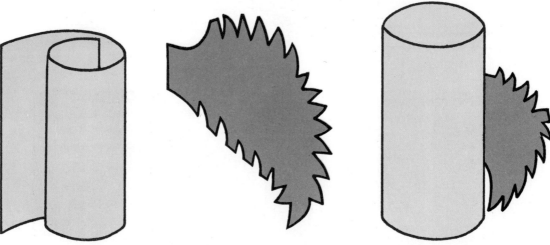

THE HEAD:

Cut this jagged pattern out of white paper. Make deep cuts round the edge.

To make the eyes, first cut a thin strip of green paper. Fold it across the middle. Curl the ends over a sharp edge. Fit the fold into the slot in the beak. Stick it on the head.

Cut long strips of brown crêpe paper and cut a jagged edge along the bottom. Wrap the strips round the owl's body and stick.

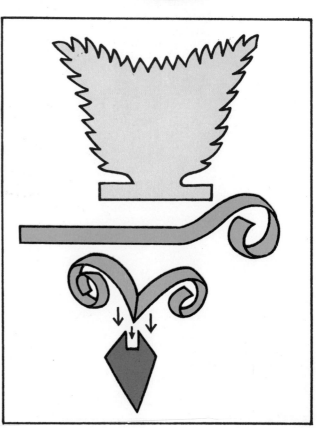

ENGINE

Cut the three pieces shown out of white paper.

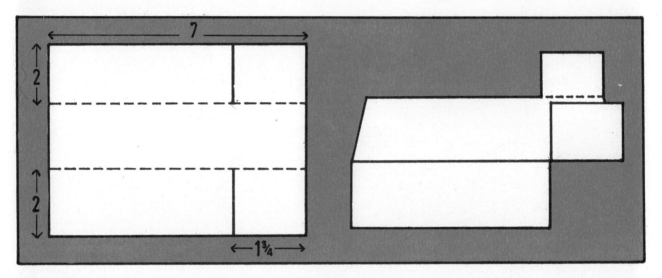

The first piece is the base of the engine. Stick the second part on the base, to make the boiler, leaving the hole for the funnel on top.

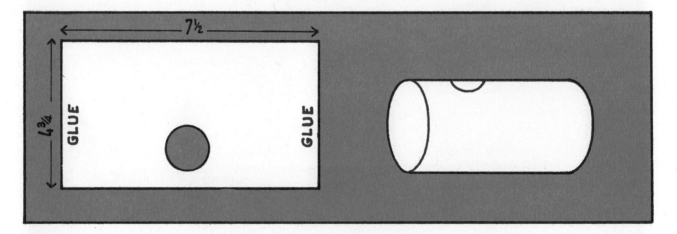

Cover the back of the boiler with the third piece and make the driver's cabin as shown. Cover the front of the boiler with a circle of paper, using the four tabs to stick it in place.

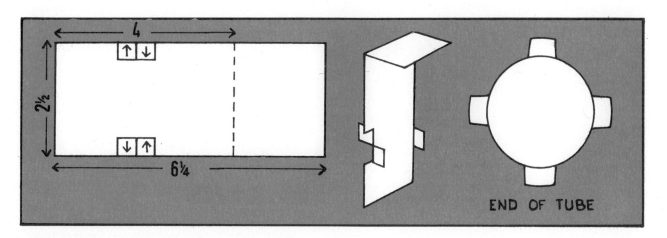

The funnel is a paper tube. The smoke is made from strips of coloured tissue paper.

BOOK MARKERS

Cut a strip of red shiny paper, longer than the book. On the part that sticks out of the book, glue a circle of pink paper for the face.

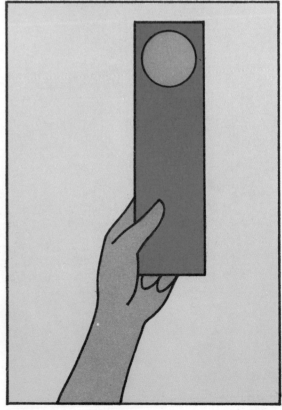

Make the eyes with white and black paper. Stick them on to the face. Then draw the feet.

LANTERN

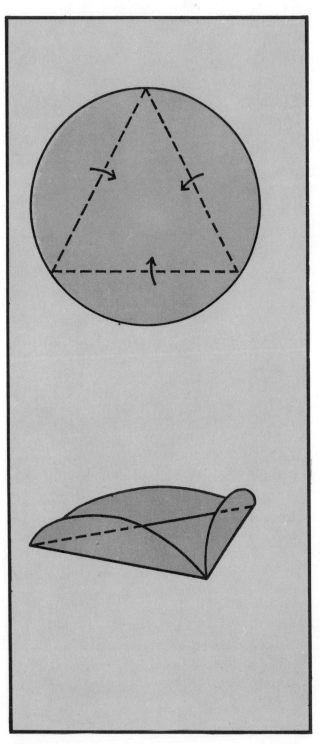

Cut out twenty circles, the same size as the one shown here.
Fold each circle upwards on the dotted lines.

You now have twenty shapes like this.

Stick them together by joining the sides so that you have five triangles meeting at each corner.

You can make other lanterns in coloured paper and hang them in one corner of a room at different heights.

COLLAGE OF BIRDS

Use the pattern below for all the birds.

The beaks are made from shiny paper. The eyes are circles of tissue paper.

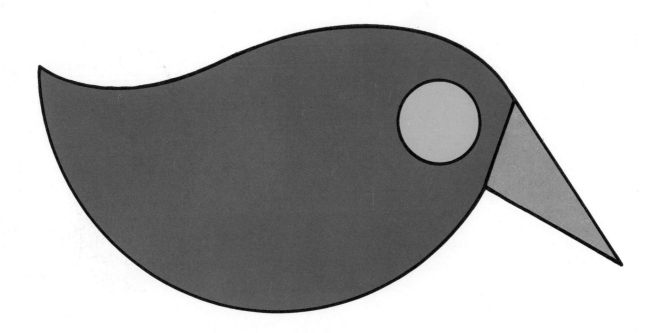

SCULPTURE

The sculpture is made of sixteen squares. Cut sixteen strips 11in. by $1\frac{1}{4}$in. out of white paper.

Cover them with coloured paper, and fold every $2\frac{1}{2}$in., leaving $\frac{1}{2}$in. either end. Stick the ends together.

Stick the squares together, using the photograph opposite as a guide.

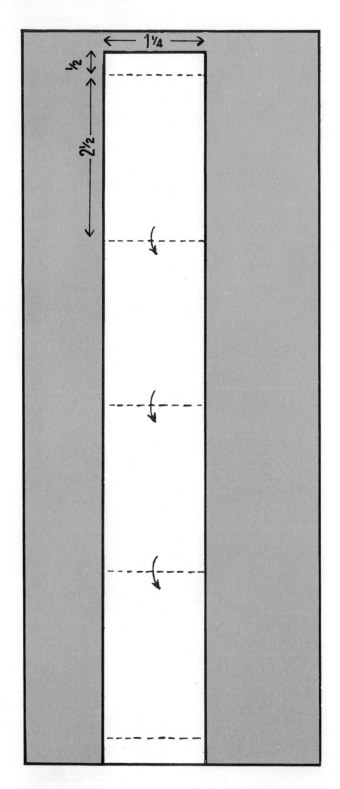

MATERIALS:

- White paper
- Silver paper
- Needle
- Compasses
- Glue
- Ruler
- Drawing pin
- Candle
- Scissors

CHINESE LANTERN

Cut a piece of paper into a rectangle about 15in. by 7½in. Make the same size rectangle in silver paper and stick it on to the white one. Draw a circle with a radius of 2½in. on a sheet of thin paper.

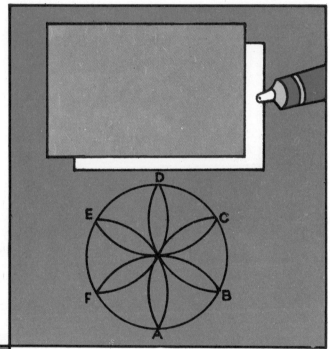

Keep the same radius and use the pair of compasses to mark off the points A,B,C,D,E and F. Put the point of the compasses at each of these marks and draw semicircles in the circle.

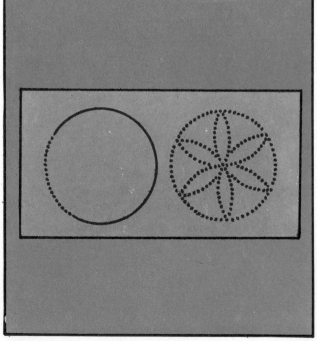

Place this drawing on the rectangle of silver paper. Pin-prick round the outline with a needle, making sure you pierce both sheets of paper.

Bend the silver paper into a cylinder and glue the ends. Cut a white strip for the handle and fold it down the middle to make it stronger. Cover it with silver paper. Stick the ends on the inside of the cylinder as shown.

Stick another strip of paper across the bottom. Push a drawing pin through the centre of this strip to hold the candle.

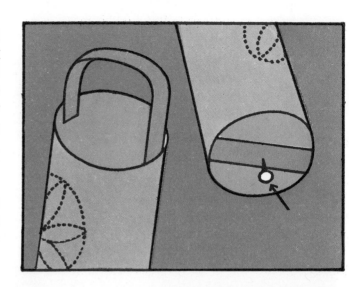

STAINED-GLASS WINDOW

Draw this pattern on black card. Cut out the parts which are white or coloured.

Cover the empty spaces by sticking on pieces of cellophane.

Brush a little glue all over the cellophane to make it look more like glass.

Put your work against a window pane. It will look like a stained-glass window.

MOBILE OF RINGS

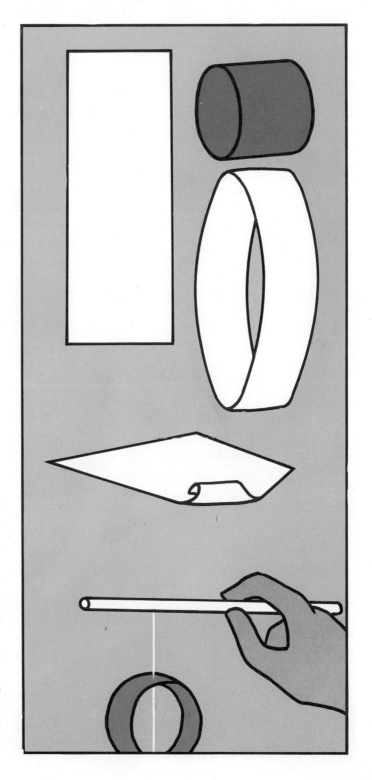

Start with the large circle in the mobile. Cut out a rectangle of white paper 15in. by 1½in. Stick the ends together.

The small circles are made from rectangles of shiny paper 5in. by 1½in.

Now take a sheet of white paper 10½in. by 15½in. Cut it in half and roll each piece diagonally from one of the corners to make the rods.

Last of all thread a needle with white cotton. Pass it through the circles and the corresponding rod. Glue the ends of cotton to the paper.
As you can see, this mobile is very easy to make. If you hang it from the ceiling near a heater it will move round.

SMALL JAPANESE LANTERN

Cut a rectangle of white paper and stick the short sides together to make a cylinder.

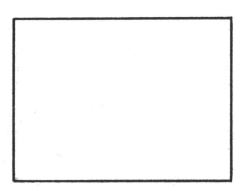

Cut another rectangle of coloured paper, about $\frac{1}{2}$in. wider than the first one.
Lightly draw in the lines shown below.
Cut along them.

Stick the uncut top and bottom edges of the coloured paper round the white cylinder.

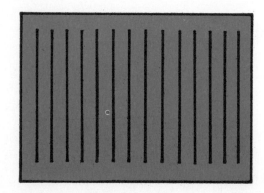

143

COLLAGE OF FLOWERS

Put the pieces of tissue paper one on top of the other and cut out the flower shape and circle shown above.

When you have enough patterns, arrange them on the white card. The example on the next page shows one way of arranging them.

Stick the patterns down carefully. This is quite difficult with such thin paper.

CROWN

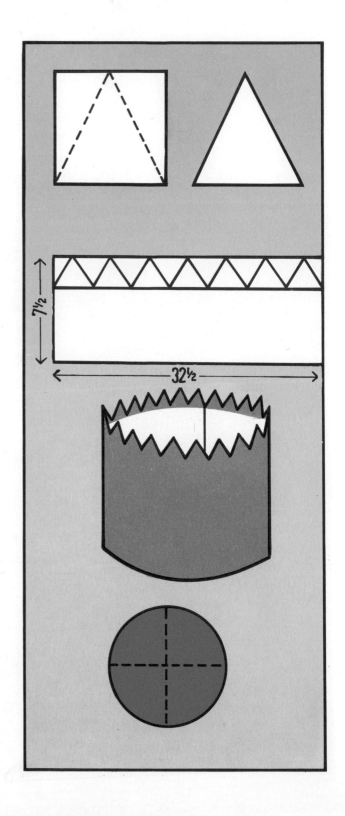

Cut a rectangle of white paper about 32½in. by 7½in. Cover one side with gold paper.

Cut a 2½in. square out of white paper.

Draw a triangle on it as shown and cut it out.

On the back of the rectangle draw a straight line 2½in. from the top. Place the triangle on the line and draw round it until you come to the end of the line.

Cut along the zig-zag line. Use the gold triangles you have cut out to cover the points of the crown on the inside.

Stick the ends of the rectangle together to make a cylinder.

Cut two strips of white paper 10in. by 1in. and two more of gold paper. Stick the white strips crosswise inside the top of the crown.

Cut a circle of pink tissue paper the same size as the base of the crown. Cut it into four.
Stick the edges of each one to the white strips.

Stick the strips of gold paper over the pink tissue paper in the same position as the white ones.

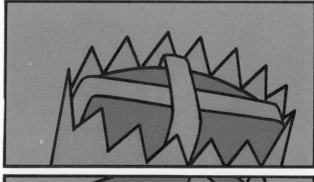

You can decorate the crown with shapes cut out of shiny paper, as shown in the photograph.

DECORATING
BOOK COVERS

To make a bright book cover you can use paper from illustrated magazines. You can also use wrapping paper covered with a bright pattern.

We suggest two patterns below.

The first is beige wrapping paper decorated with triangles of shiny brown and yellow paper.
The second is white paper decorated with semicircles of shiny blue and red paper.

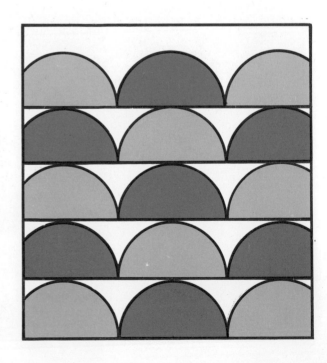

149

MASK

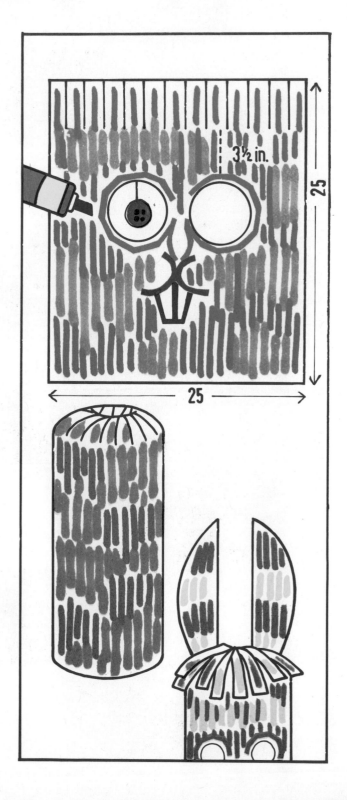

Cut a 25in. square out of white paper. Make cuts along the top 5in. deep and 1in. apart. Cut out the eyes and draw circles round them with a felt-tip pen. Draw the nose and the teeth.

Thread each button on to a piece of cotton. Stick the ends of the cotton with sticky tape on the inside of the mask so the buttons show in the eye holes.

Fold the strips round the top of the mask inwards and stick them together. Cut out the ears of the rabbit and stick them on.

Stick strips of shiny yellow and orange paper on to the head so that it falls over the forehead for the hair.

The whiskers are strips of brown paper glued on either side of the face.

Decorate the rabbit with coloured felt-tip pens.

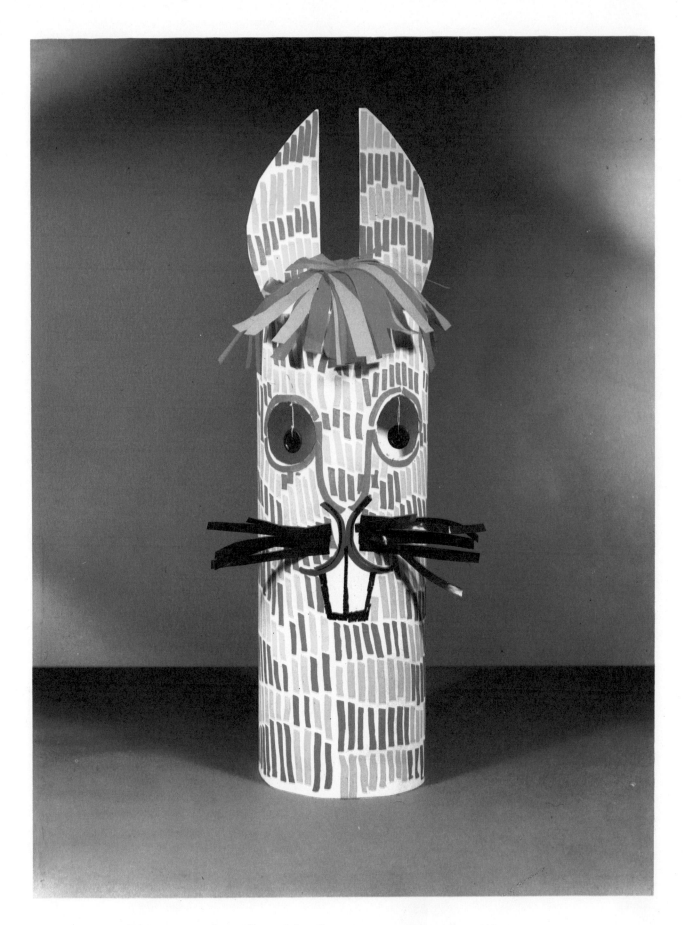

Put the mask on your head and let it rest on your shoulders.

Cut two small circles level with your eyes so that you can see out.

MATERIALS:

- White paper
- Shiny paper
- Tissue paper
- Magazine pages
- Ball-point pen
- Scissors
- Glue

VIRGIN MARY

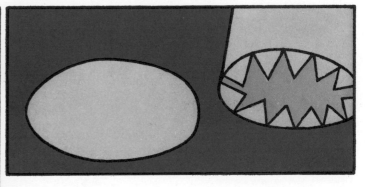

PEDESTAL:

Cut a rectangle about 10in. by 7½in. Cut a zig-zag along the top. Stick the two ends A and B together. Flatten the tube slightly at either side so that it is not quite round. Fold the zig-zag points inwards. Stick the oval shape shown above on the bottom.

VIRGIN MARY:

Make another cylinder from a slightly smaller rectangle.
Stick on the face, which is made from shiny pink paper.
Draw in the eyes, nose and mouth with a ball-point pen.

CLOAK:

Cut a rectangle 15in. by 2½in. Stick it to the sides of the pedestal. Decorate it with flowers made from blue tissue paper.

HALO:

Draw three overlapping circles with a radius of 2½in. as shown on the right and cut round the outline. Decorate the halo with orange and pink tissue paper.

CHILD:

Cut a rectangle 2½in. by 1½in. and cover with brightly coloured paper. Glue the long sides together. Use strips of yellow tissue paper for the hair.

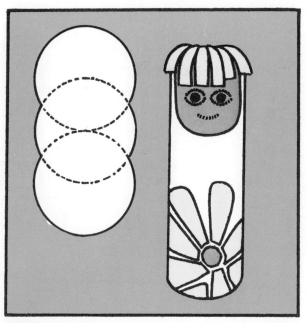

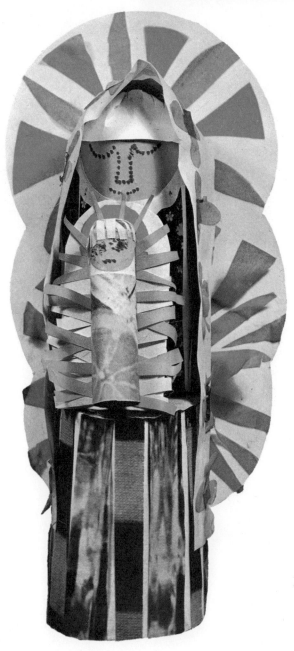

WRAPPING & DECORATING PARCELS

Spread out a sheet of silver paper on the table.
Put the box you are going to wrap in the centre.

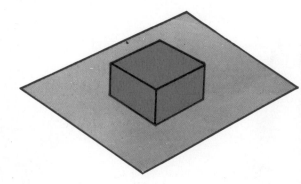

Follow the instructions given in the diagrams.

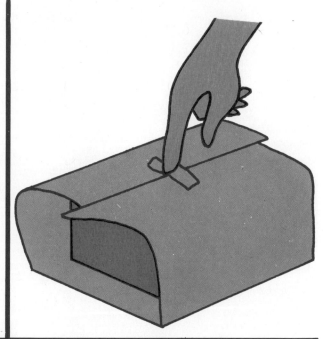

Make the folds neatly and firmly.

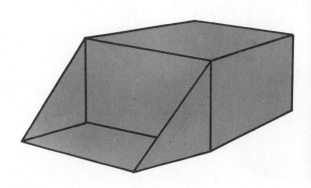

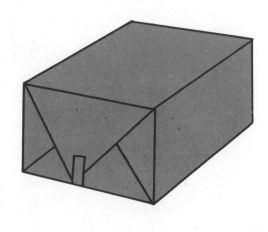

Once you have wrapped the parcel, decorate it like the one in the photograph.

BIRD

Cut a rectangle of white paper 11in. by 2½in.
Stick the ends together to make the body of the bird. Make two holes in it as shown.

Make a tube by cutting a strip of paper 10in. long and rolling it round a pencil. Stick the edge down and remove the pencil.

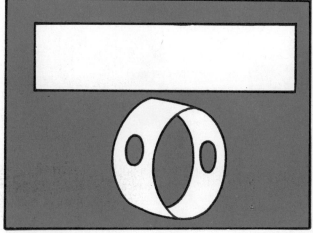

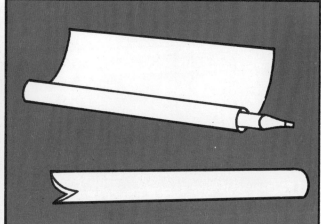

Cut 2½in. squares in different colours. Cut a zig-zag across the top and stick one on top of the other until you have covered the body.

Make a cut in the tube so that it looks like a beak. Cover the tube with coloured paper.

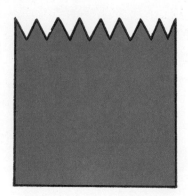

Push the tube through the holes in the cylinder. To make the tail, cut strips of coloured paper and stick them to the back end of the tube. The eyes are made from circles of paper.

LARGE PAPER FLOWER

Cut a long strip of white crêpe paper about 10in. wide. Make folds every 7½in. in the direction of the arrows.

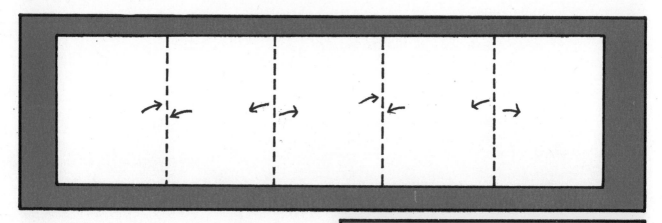

Draw an outline on the folded paper, like the one on the right.

If you cut round this outline you will get several petals joined together.

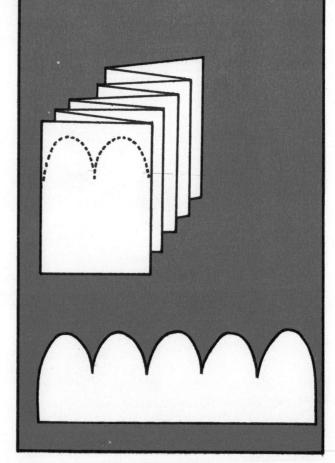

Cut a strip of yellow crêpe paper a bit shorter than the previous one, but the same width. Cut a fringe along the top.

Bunch the strip together and bind with thin wire to make the centre of the flower.

Wrap the white petals round the centre and bind with another piece of wire. Cover the bottom with green crêpe paper. Make the stalk with a slightly thicker piece of wire covered in green crêpe paper.
On the following pages you will find instructions for making two more flowers and a photograph of some finished examples.

BUNCH OF FLOWERS

Make these flowers in the same way as the one on the previous page.

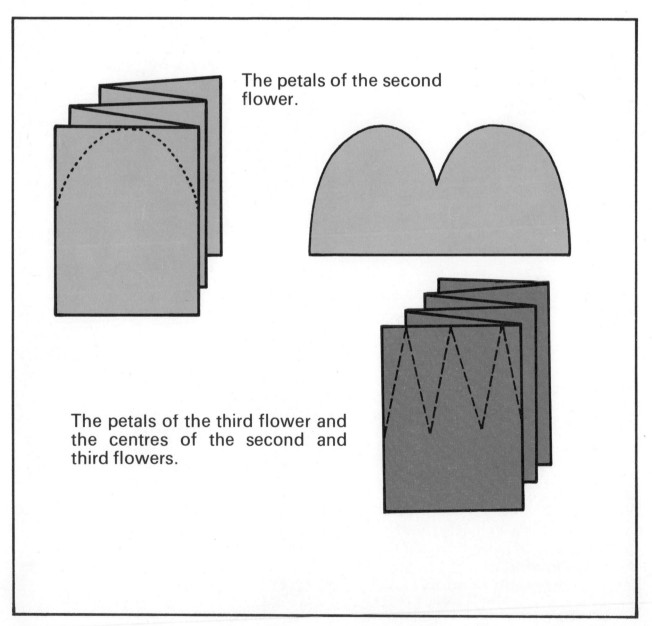

The petals of the second flower.

The petals of the third flower and the centres of the second and third flowers.

HELICOPTER

Make the tubes for this helicopter by rolling fairly wide sheets of paper round a pencil. Then stick the outside edge down and remove the pencil.

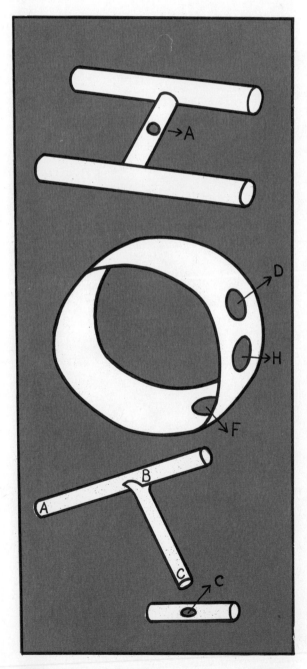

THE UNDERCARRIAGE:

Two large tubes of paper 8in. long.
A small tube 3½in. long. Make a hole in the long tubes and glue the ends of the short one into them.

THE CABIN:

A rectangle 11½in. by 2½in. Join the ends to make the shapes shown in the diagram. Then make three holes as indicated.

THE VERTICAL TUBE:

8in. long. Glue end A of the vertical tube into hole A in the undercarriage, passing it through holes D and F in the cabin.

THE TAIL:

6½in. long. Make a cut at one end and glue the two flaps to the vertical tube at B, after slotting it into the cabin through H

THE REAR VERTICAL: TUBE:

2½in. long. Insert end C of the tail tube into hole C.

THE BLADES:

Long: two strips 13in. by $\frac{3}{4}$in. stuck together.
Short: two strips $2\frac{1}{2}$in. by $\frac{1}{2}$in. stuck together.

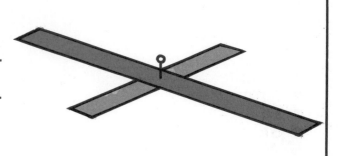

The model can be decorated with coloured felt-tip pens.

COLLAGE OF SHAPES

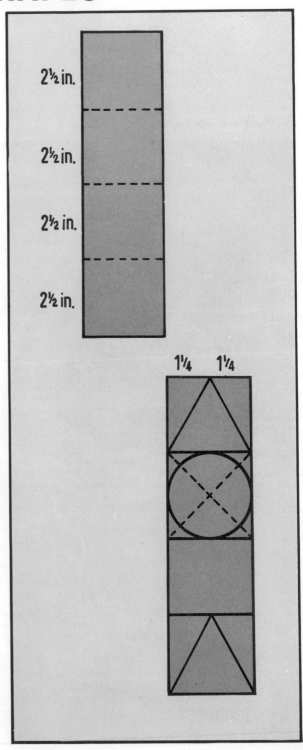

Cut eight different coloured strips of paper 10in. by 2½in.

Divide the first strip into four parts. Mark the divisions lightly in pencil. You now have four 2½in. squares.

Draw a triangle with a 2½in. base.

Draw a circle. Its centre is the point where the diagonals of the square cross.

The square has already been drawn.

Draw a triangle like the first one.

Place the strip you have drawn on top of the pile of other strips, and cut out all the shapes in one cutting.

164

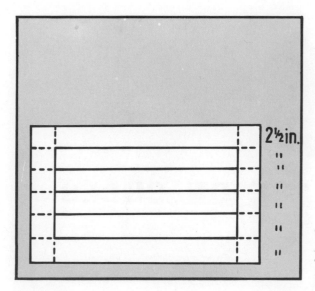

Take a sheet of white or black card
25in. long and 15in. wide.
Divide it up as shown on the left.

Place the paper shapes on the card. Arrange them as shown below. Stick them on with a little glue.

COLLAGE ON CUBES

TO MAKE THE CUBE:

Draw the figure shown below.
There are six $2\frac{1}{2}$in. squares. Fold on the dotted lines, following the direction of the arrows.

Glue A to A, B to B, and C to C, etc.

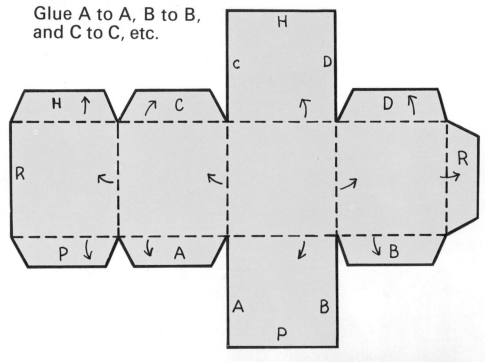

TO DECORATE THE CUBES:

Make four cubes like the first one. Stick photographs cut out from magazines on two opposite sides of each cube.

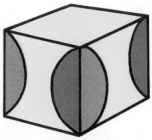
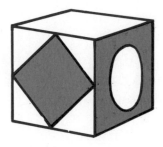

You can also use patterns of opposites. For instance, if one side has a red circle on a white background, its opposite would be a white circle on a red background.

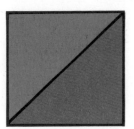

Here are some more patterns you can copy.

BOAT

To make the BASE of the boat, trace the shape below on to paper. Cut it out. Fold the jagged edges upwards.

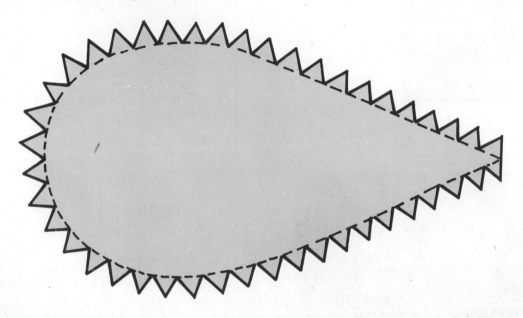

Cut a rectangle 15in. by 3in. Bend it as shown on the right, and glue it to the jagged edges of the base.

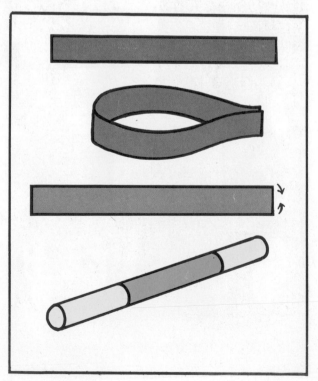

FUNNEL:

Cut a rectangle 5in. by 3in. Make a long tube and cover with coloured paper.

MAST:

Roll a piece of paper 8in. wide round a pencil.

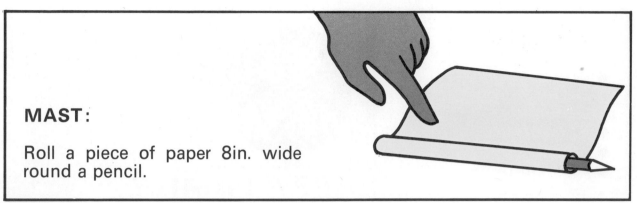

BRIDGE:

Measure out the pattern shown below on a sheet of newspaper.
Fold it on the dotted lines and stick the bottom edges of the sides to the inside of the boat.

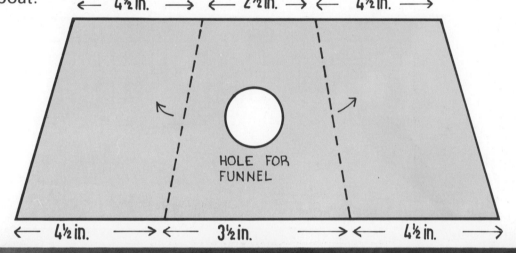

← 4½ in. →   ← 2½ in. →   ← 4½ in. →

HOLE FOR FUNNEL

← 4½ in. →   ← 3½ in. →   ← 4½ in. →

Cut a hole for the funnel. Now decorate the boat.

MATERIALS:

- White paper
- Different coloured paper
- Scissors
- Glue
- Felt-tip pens

HIPPY FAMILY

Cut a rectangle of paper 13in. by 6¾in. Glue the two ends together to make a tube. Make cuts round the top part and fold the flaps inwards. Some will overlap. Stick them together.

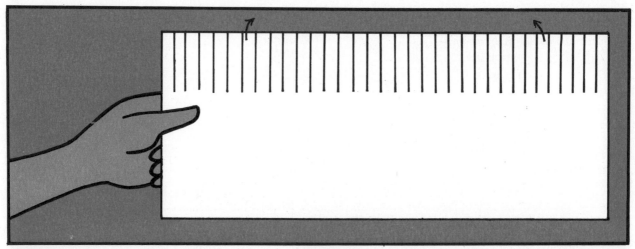

CAP:

Cut a circle of coloured paper 4in. in diameter. Make a slit to the centre and overlap edges A and B to make a pointed cap.

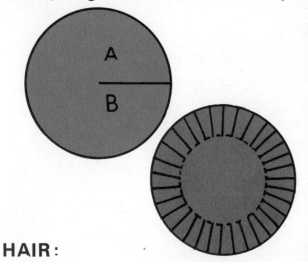

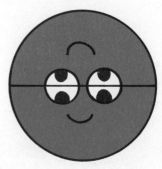

FACE:

Cut a circle of pink paper 5in. in diameter.
If you cut it down the middle you will have two faces.
Draw them in with felt-tip pens and stick them under the hair.

HAIR:

Cut a circle of coloured paper 4in. in diameter. Stick it on to the head.
Cut a fringe round the edge so that it falls over the face.

BASE:

Cut a circle of coloured paper a bit larger than the base of the tube. Cut the outer edge in a zig-zag and fold the points upwards.

Cut a strip of paper 13½in. by 1½in. Stick it round the outside of the points of the circle.

The length of the rectangles for the bodies of the other figures should get smaller by 1½in. in each case. The height should decrease by 1in. You can work out the other measurements yourself. Lastly decorate all the figures with felt-tip pens. They should all fit inside each other, and the largest one sits in the base.

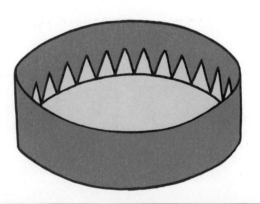

BIRD

Fold a sheet of paper the same way as for the pirana fish on page 66 until you have the small table.

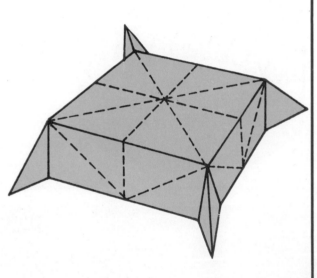

Now turn the table upside down, folding the corners to point in the same direction.

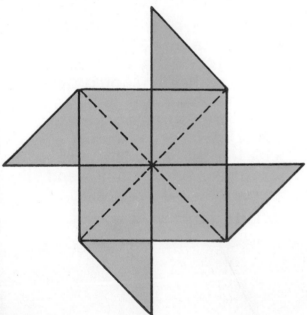

Fold the shape diagonally backwards, leaving two opposite corners free.

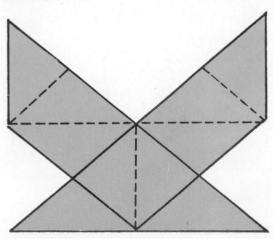

Join the two corners of the base. You now have a sailing boat.

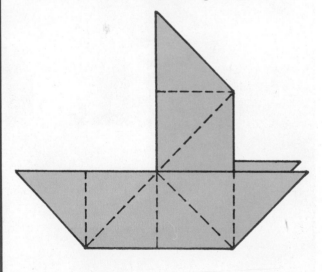

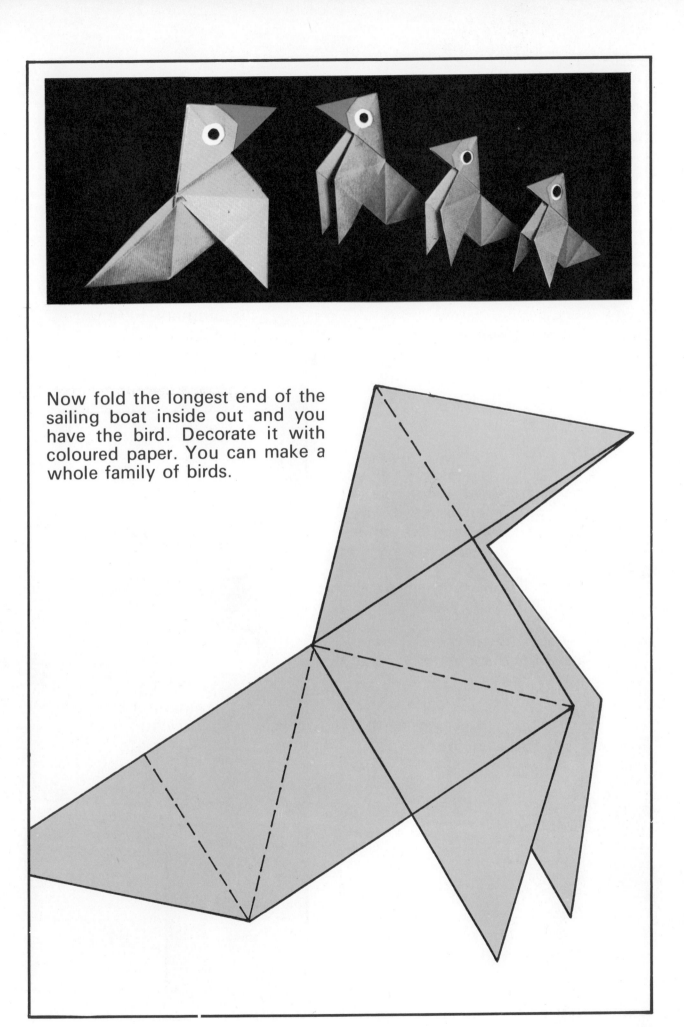

Now fold the longest end of the sailing boat inside out and you have the bird. Decorate it with coloured paper. You can make a whole family of birds.

JET PLANE

These pictures show you how to make the parts of the jet plane.

BODY:

Cut a rectangle of white paper 7½in. by 5in. Then make it into a tube by sticking the ends together.

Make a small cone of white paper and trim the bottom edge.

Join point A of the cone to point A of the tube. Stick them together with sticky tape.

Make a thin tube of white paper. Fix it to tip B with glue.

Decorate these three parts with coloured paper.

174

ENGINES:

These are two tubes 5in. in length, decorated with coloured paper.

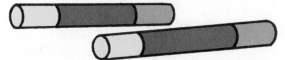

Make two more tubes a little shorter than the first two.

To make the WINGS cut a 6½in. square out of white paper. Fold it in half. Cut the shape shown on the right from the triangle you have made.

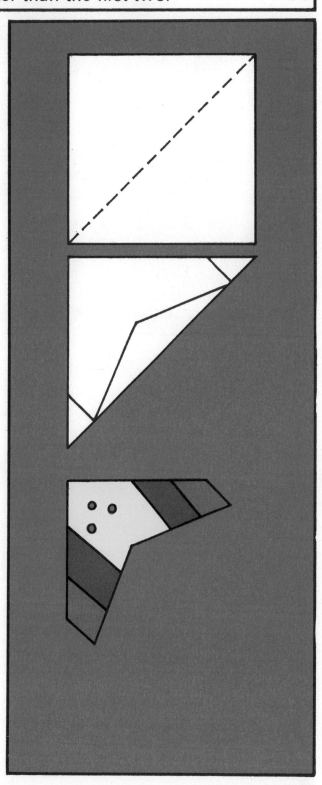

Place the shape you have cut out on a piece of cardboard.
Draw round the edge and cut the cardboard.

Make three small holes in the cardboard. Decorate the wings and stick them to the other parts you have already made.

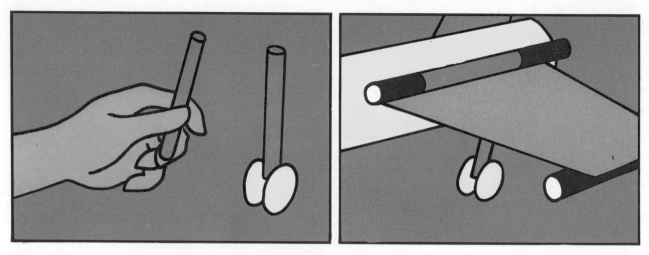

UNDERCARRIAGE:

Make this with three thin, short tubes. Insert them in the holes on the wings and add wheels made from coloured paper.

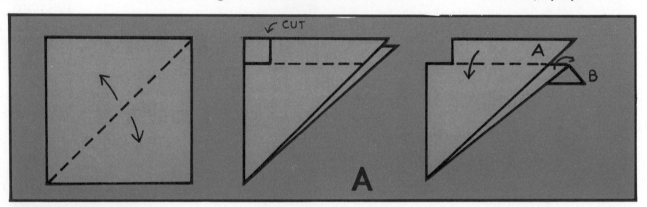

RUDDER:

This is made up of parts A and B.

A) Square a sheet of paper and fold it as shown above. Cut out the square corner as shown and fold out parts A and B. Glue them on to the body of the jet.

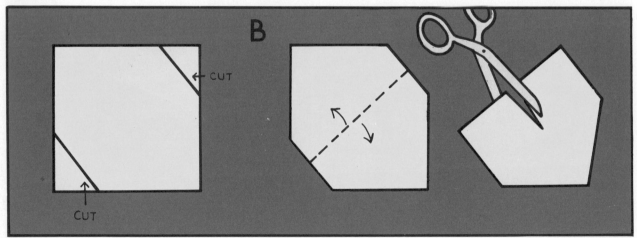

B) Cut out the shape shown above.
Fold on the dotted line and cut as shown. Join this piece to piece A as shown opposite. Now you have the tailpiece. Decorate it as shown in the photograph.

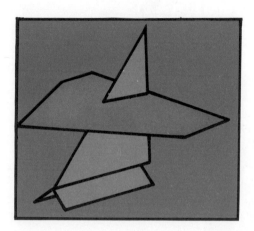

Now cut out letters and numbers from a magazine or newspaper and stick them on to the jet.

KITES

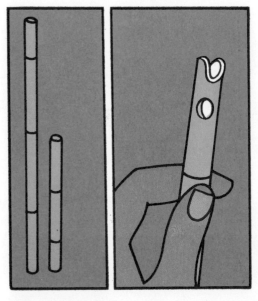

To make the framework of the kite cut two lengths of cane. One should be twice as long as the other. Use a knife to make a groove at either end of the rods and bore a hole just below it. Cross these rods so that the distances OA, OB and OC, are equal. Then run a piece of string through the grooves, keeping it taut. Knot the ends of the string together.

Place the frame on a sheet of coloured paper. Cut the paper as shown, fold it, and glue over the cane.

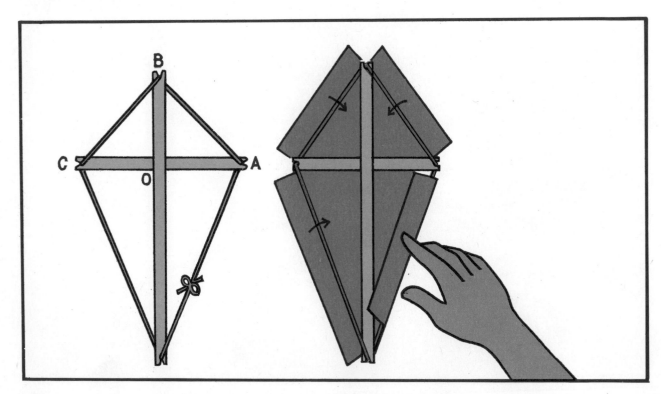

Carefully make two holes in the paper at the point where you made holes in the rods. Thread some thin string through them as shown below. Try to keep the distances AC, AD, and AB equal.

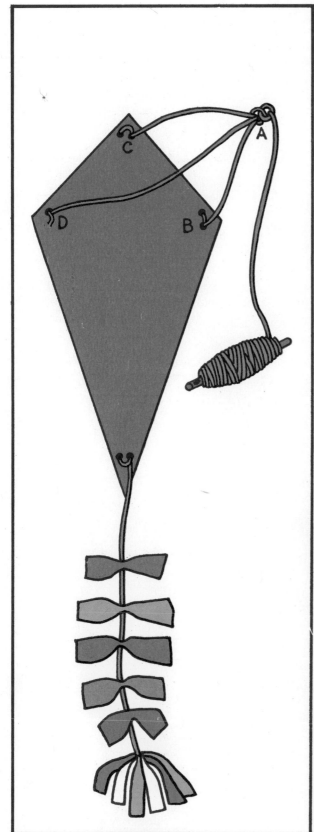

Perhaps the most attractive part of a kite is the tail.

You can make it by tying pieces of coloured material to a piece of string attached to the bottom of the kite. This is shown in the picture below.

Finish the tail with a tassel of strips of coloured material.

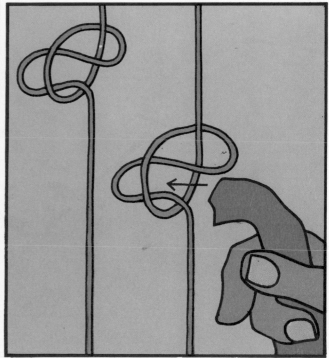

DECORATING KITES

PANEL OF SUNS

This panel is very simple. It is made by cutting circles of different colours and sizes, and then arranging them as shown on the opposite page.

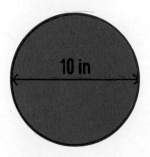

Cut a circle about 10in. in diameter out of brown paper. Cut another circle the same size out of yellow paper. Draw a ten-pointed star on the yellow circle and cut it out.

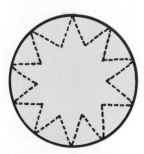

Cut another circle in orange paper. Make it a little smaller than the others, so that it does not hide the points of the yellow star.
Stick a small red circle in the middle of the orange one.

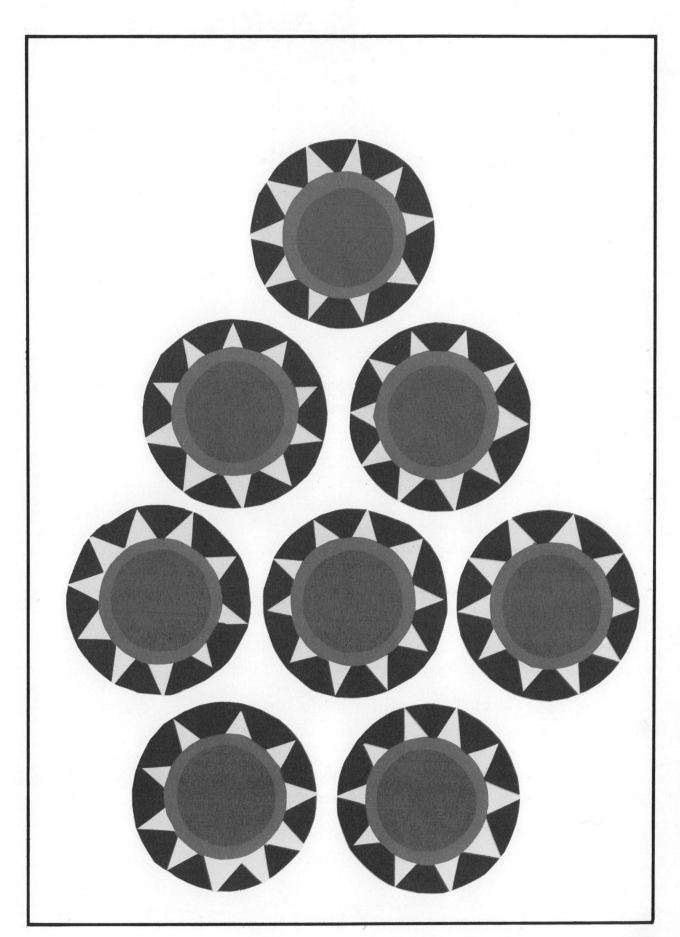

MATERIALS:

● White paper
● Pink and purple tissue paper
● Black paper
● Scissors
● Glue

HANGING FISH

Cut seven strips of pink tissue paper about ¾in. by 2½in. Then cut seven purple strips the same size.

The skeleton of the fish is made from three strips of white paper which have the following measurements:
One strip 20in. by 2½in.
Two strips 37½in. by 2½in.
Make these strips into three circles.

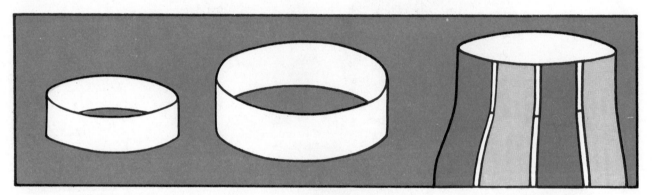

Glue the pink strips on to one of the large circles one after the other. The top ends must overlap the circle by an equal amount to make the head.

Leave a space and then glue the strips in exactly the same way to the other large circle.
Stick the top ends of the strips on to the small circle overlapping them in pairs.

Tie the bottom ends of the strips together with a green strip as shown in the photograph.

The eyes are two white circles with a black circle in the middle.

Hang the fish on a thin string. The breeze will make it swing out sideways.

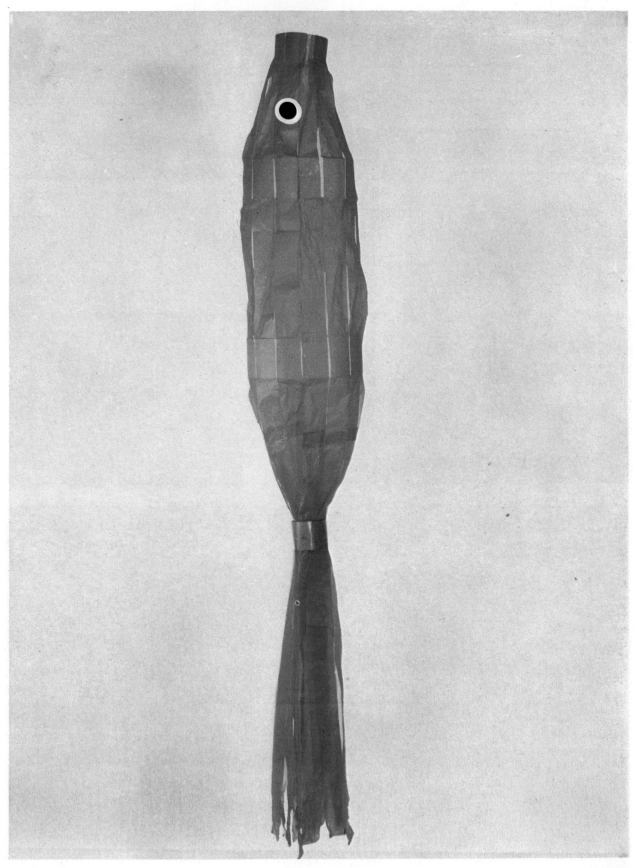

CELLOPHANE BUTTERFLIES

Fold a rectangle of white paper in half. Draw half a butterfly like the one on the left. Cut on the lines.

Open out the paper. Cover the spaces by sticking on pieces of coloured cellophane.

Make several butterflies like this.

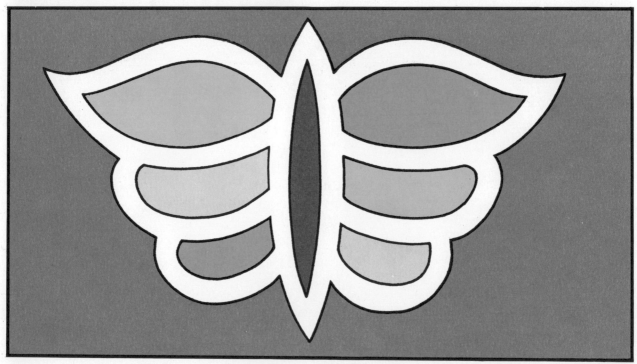

Stick the butterflies on to a sheet of cardboard. Then cover the whole thing with clear cellophane.

MATERIALS:

● A large sheet of
  white cardboard
● Coloured paper
● Scissors
● Glue
● Compasses
● Ruler

COLLAGE

Draw a 20in. square on a large sheet of cardboard.
Divide each side of the square into eight parts and square it off as shown.

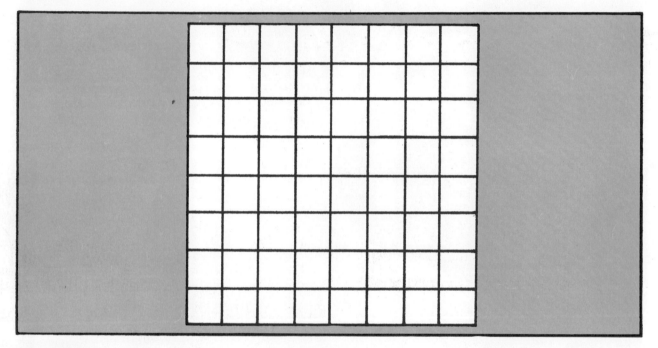

Find some pieces of paper in the colours shown on the right.
Cut twelve 2½in. squares from each colour. Stick them on to the cardboard as follows:

First row across: Bright yellow, dark yellow, orange, red, grey, green, blue, black.

Second row across: Begin with the black and finish with the yellow.

Thrid row: The same as the first. Fill the other rows in the same way, alternating the order of colours.

You have four squares of each colour left. In each one draw a circle with a 1¼in. radius and then halve it. Stick these semicircles on to one half of each of the squares.

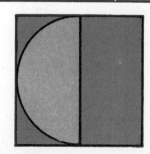

The order of colours for the semicircles is the reverse of the one you used for the squares.

INDEX